My Breaking Point

Copyright © 2017 by E.M.E.R.G.E. Youth Development Foundation
c/o Deunta Williams

Book Cover Design by Emmanuel Gonzales
Interior Formatting by Type A Formatting

A CIP catalog record for this book is available from the Library of Congress.

Williams, Deunta
My Breaking Point / by Deunta Williams—First edition

My Breaking Point may be purchased for educational, business, and sales promotional use. For information, please e-mail Deunta Williams at pro.deuntawilliams@gmail.com. Visit his website at: DeuntaWilliams.com

ISBN-13: 978–0-9992639–0-7 (paperback)
ISBN-13: 978–0-9992639–1-4 (ebook)

Made in the USA
10 9 8 7 6 5 4 3 2 1

My Breaking Point

Deunta Williams

PUBLISHING
HOUSE

This book is dedicated to my family and the city of Jacksonville, NC
I am a product of J-Ville and Onslow County

I also dedicate this book to
all of those who have fallen but found a way to get back up

Thank you from the bottom of my heart

CONTENTS

Foreward: My Mother

Chapter 1:   Introduction: My Breaking Point

Chapter 2:   Adversity: The Road to Neverland

Chapter 3:   Growth: Lessons Learned

Chapter 4:   Practicing the Power of Courage:
                     Advice From the Sideline

Afterword: Big Ticket Out of the Hood

Acknowledgements

About the Author

Notes

Index

HIGH SCHOOL AND COLLEGE HONORS

WHITE OAK HIGH SCHOOL

- Defensive MVP for the Shrine Bowl of the Carolinas
- Scholarship to the University of North Carolina

UNIVERSITY OF NORTH CAROLINA

- *FWAA* and *Rivals.com* Freshman All-American, 2007
- *TSN* First-Team All-ACC Freshman, 2007
- ACC Defensive Rookie of the Year, 2007
- First-Team All-ACC, 2009

COLLEGE STATISTICS AT
THE UNIVERSITY OF NORTH CAROLINA

| Classification | | | Tackles | | | INT |
Year	Class	Games	Solo	AST	TOT	TOT
2007	FR	12	39	18	57	3
2008	SO	13	55	10	65	3
2009	JR	13	34	13	47	6
2010	SR	9	30	19	49	0

ATHLETIC PROFILE OF DEUNTA WILLIAMS

University of North Carolina
Defensive Back—Safety

2011 PRE-DRAFT COMBINE RANKING: 4.88/5.00
HEIGHT: 6'2"
ARM LENGTH: 33 ¼"
WEIGHT: 205 lbs
HANDS: 10"

OVERVIEW: Williams is a supremely confident safety who has the speed and cover skills to eventually develop into a starter at the next level. He puts in time in the film room and always appears to be in position to make a play in coverage. He has the speed to be a true center fielder and the terrific hands to make acrobatic interceptions. He must become more physical in run support, but he takes proper angles to the ball and makes tackles despite not delivering big shots on impact. Williams has a chance to sneak into the second round if he runs really well.

STRENGTHS: Williams has ideal size and good speed. Smart kid that is always in position and shows a knack for anticipating routes. Fluid athlete that sticks with receivers in and out of their breaks in man coverage. Possesses reliable hands and the body control to make difficult interceptions. Takes precise angles in run support and is a sound tackler.

WEAKNESSES: Over-aggressive at times and can be burned by double moves. Lacks physicality in run support and struggles to disengage from blockers. Does not deliver violent shots when tackling and will sometimes resort to arm tackles. Will not make plays in jump ball situations.

SOURCE: NFL.com[1]

FOREWARD

Dear Deunta,

I love you, son. I am very proud of you for writing this book and telling your story.

I remember the day you were born. I never knew true love *until I held you* in my arms and looked into your eyes for the very *first time. It was at that moment,* I really felt in my heart the meaning of real love. You captured my mind, body, and soul! I felt a love that I never knew existed. Your mere presence paralyzed me. I was your mother and you were my son. I knew then that I could and would move Heaven and Earth for you and no one or no thing could ever stop me!

I admire your perseverance. As a mother, it is difficult to see our child endure a breaking point. But as I have always told you, "Adversity causes some to break, but it causes others to break through."

Love,
Your Mother

CHAPTER 1
INTRODUCTION: MY BREAKING POINT

James 1:12 reads, "Blessed is the one who perseveres under trial because, having stood the test, that person will receive the crown of life that the Lord has promised to those who love him."

December 30, 2010, a cold, icy day in Nashville, TN. The last time I would ever play football.

"Bang!"

"Ahhhhhhhhhh!" My body instantly contorted as I screamed in pain while making a tackle in the 2010 Franklin American Mortgage Music City Bowl against the Tennessee Volunteers. Only 9:28 into the first quarter of my last college football game, I had broken my right fibula at the ankle joint while assisting on a tackle of Volunteers tight end, Luke Stocker.

Grimacing in pain, I laid there. I could hear players around me in a panic saying, "Come out! Come out!" to the athletic trainers. Lying on the field as trainers waved for a cart and to place my lower right leg in a brace, I immediately began to think that my childhood dream of playing in the National Football League (NFL) was over. I laid on the field as an athlete who was promised to be one of the top picks in the upcoming 2011 NFL draft; however, in a matter of seconds left to question whether I would ever play competitive football again. In this moment, a lot of thoughts were running through my mind.

I thought about my teammates. I did not want to fail them. Although we had a disappointing year following a National Collegiate Athletic Association (NCAA) investigation that led to the suspension of some of our best players, I honestly believed we could have been one of the best teams in college football. I had faith we could have possibly won a national championship, which was one of the main reasons for returning to play my senior year.

I thought about my grandmother, who I call "Nana." I remembered telling her that after being drafted into the NFL, I would buy her a home.

I thought about my mother. She had worked extremely hard to provide for our family. In return, I wanted to continue making her proud. My mother always wanted to be the mom in the Campbell's Chunky Soup commercials like so many other mothers of professional athletes.

I thought about my Uncle Henry. My Nana, my mother, and my uncle, as a collective group, were able to mold me into a man.

I thought about losing access to the big American Dream. Twelve or more years of hard work and dedication were invested into a sport, only to end this way.

I thought about my hometown of Jacksonville, NC. I loved them and they loved me back. I wanted them to be proud of me as well.

Lastly, I thought about all of the people who had supported me to this point in my life and also wanted to see my dream of playing professional football come true.

The night before the game, I had visualized myself making key plays at important moments to help our team win the game. I am big on visualization. I believe that it helps you achieve what you are trying to accomplish by mentally priming your mind to see things in a positive way before they actually happen. I am a big dreamer, who lives for big moments, so I envisioned myself having 11 solo tackles, 5 assist tackles, 3 interceptions, and returning one for a touchdown. Although I had the most interceptions on the team, the fellas always joked with me because I had never returned one for a touchdown. If I were to get one in college, December 30, 2010 would be the day! I would be the MVP of the Music City Bowl, end my college football career on a good note, and upgrade my NFL draft stock. All of this would take place against the Tennessee Volunteers in Nashville, TN at the Tennessee Titans stadium. The stars were aligned and I planned to be the biggest star of them all.

Even more important than individual achievements, I envisioned a big bowl game win. This was not just a normal bowl game. It was the last bowl game for us as seniors on the University of North Carolina (UNC) Tar Heels football team. We had been 0–2 in bowl games since I first arrived in 2006 as a freshman. We lost in 2008 in the Meineke Car Care Bowl (L 31–30) to the West Virginia Mountaineers, and in 2009 in the Meineke Car Care Bowl (L 19–17) to the Pittsburgh Panthers. The seniors were a close-knit group; therefore, it was important for us to leave UNC with at least one bowl game win under our belts in a glorious send off.

I was wincing in pain as all of these things were running through my mind as the trainers carted me off of the field. During halftime, I told my homeboy and roommate, Kendric Burney, who was also from Jacksonville, "[W]in this [game] for [the seniors]."[2] In the locker room, the medical staff took an x-ray of my right leg to confirm the break. I could not feel my right leg. I could not feel my right foot.

To make matters worse, I could not return to the sidelines to cheer my teammates on. And my former head coach, Butch Davis, had a strict policy about radios and TVs in the locker room. It was his son, Drew Davis, who kept going back and forth and reporting the score of the game to me. All I heard from the locker room were the oohh's and aahh's of the crowd. Finally, the team rushed into the locker room victorious. We had won 30–27 in double-overtime. The win was bittersweet for me.

★ ★ ★

"North Carolina Safety Deunta Williams has surgery on broken leg," was the headline reported by many local and national media outlets. Dr. Tim Taft, who performed the surgery at UNC Hospitals, and the folks at UNC were optimistic that I would make a full recovery. Coach Davis told local reporters, "The good news is that it's something that's going to be fixable."[3] Despite the outpour of optimism, I knew the road back to being the player I was before the injury would be difficult. I rehabbed every day—two to three hours a day. When the doctor removed the screw from my lower right leg, I worked extremely hard to get back on the playing field.

During this time, I was extremely grateful for the support of my agent, Eugene Parker, and UNC for their care during the recovery process. Both stood by their word when they told me that they would make sure I was well taken care of.

Heading into the NFL scouting combine in 2011, I was ranked as one of the best defensive backs in NCAA college football. Before the injury, I was rated as high as the #1 defensive back on some NFL draft boards. The NFL scouting combine, which is a sporting event that through different drills and performance measures the athletic ability and skill of potential draft picks, rated me high as well. The NFL combine website rated me at 4.88 on a 5.00 point scale and described me as a, "[S]upremely confident safety who has the speed and cover skills to eventually develop into a starter at the next level."[4] Many NFL football scouts projected me as a late first-round or early second-round pick. I knew in the back of my mind that the injury could change my fate from late first-round to early second-round lock to leaving some NFL teams to question whether or not I was even worth spending a draft pick on.

Furthermore, my statistical output was low in my senior year due to being suspended by the NCAA and having to miss the first four games for allegedly receiving "preferential treatment." Despite this, there were NFL teams who still believed I could return to form and make a huge contribution to their organization. I finished my senior season with 49 tackles, three pass breakups, and no interceptions. Previously, in my junior and sophomore years, I had recorded a high number of tackles (112) along with a total of nine interceptions. Even with the suspension, statistical drop-off, and injury, NFL teams continued to show interest right up until the day of the draft.

At the NFL combine, a reporter asked me about the status of the injury. I answered, "The recovery is going excellent. I have great range of motion. I'm getting my strength back day-by-day. Each day it gets a little bit stronger. I can walk a little bit better, walk a little bit faster."[5] He then proceeded to ask about how I envisioned myself being utilized in the NFL as a safety. I explained that, "I see [myself] as more of a hybrid [type of safety who can play either at the line or in coverage] . . . my whole career at Carolina I've been kind of a head hunter for the ball and on certain running backs. I don't really mind mixing it up."[6]

During the combine, NFL team doctors checked the status of the injury. The doctors initially told me the injury was healing well, and that they saw nothing wrong on the x-ray. A month later I went back to the combine facility for a medical recheck, which is standard procedure for those athletes hurt when they arrived at the scouting combine. At the recheck, the doctors did not like the way the injury was healing. My medical records were sent to all the NFL teams. Despite the looming doubt, a sliver of hope came back when a NFL defensive back coach spoke to me during lunch and said, "I don't know how things will turn out for you. But no matter if you get drafted or not, things will work out for you because you seem like a good kid and have your head on straight."

I continued to be on such an exuberant high before the 2011 NFL draft. Family and friends were checking in with me constantly to gauge my excitement and to ask what team would possibly select me. I watched the TV listening to commentators discussing the value of drafting me and by how selecting me would meet a need in the defensive secondary for a number of NFL teams. With a NFL combine rating of 4.88 on a five point scale, surely one team would call my name on draft day.

It was my agent, Eugene, one of the most influential black agents in professional sports, who kept it real with me on the phone the day before the draft and explained that a lot of NFL teams would be weary to select me due to the injury. When I received that call from him, my heart sunk into my stomach. Maybe I was stuck in "La La Land." It was my faith in God that led me to believe that He would not have brought me this far just to leave me or forsake me. Not like this.

I had a lot of respect for Eugene who imparted great advice. When he spoke, I listened. He provided sound and significant advice on life and finances. Thus, I was too embarrassed to tell Eugene, at the time, that I had just gone to the dealership and bought a brand new Tahoe Denali SUV. Among other things, I also had people coming into town, put them up in hotels, and planned to host a "Draft Party Barbecue." My pride would not let me tell Eugene that in the euphoria of the moment.

Unfortunately, during the 2011 NFL draft, I did not hear the name

"Deunta Williams" called from the podium in New York City, NY. I watched the draft in anticipation at home in Jacksonville surrounded by family and friends. As a group, we prayed before the draft asking God for a favorable outcome. Each time the phone rang, my mother jumped with excitement. But each ring was like a dagger. Each phone call and text message during the draft was like going from 0 to 100, and then back down to 0. After each phone call my mother would say, "It's all in God's hands now."

I never shared the conversation had with Eugene the day before the draft. After the call from him, I got down on my knees and begged God to please see past all of my personal flaws and bless me with the sound of hearing my name being called during the NFL draft.

During the three-day draft from April 28 to April 30, 2011, I thought I would hear my name called. The first selection was Auburn Tiger quarterback, Cam Newton, to the North Carolina Panthers.

At Number. 2—Von Miller went to the Denver Broncos.
At Number. 3—Marcell Dareus went to the Buffalo Bills.
At Number. 4—A.J. Green went to the Cincinnati Bengals.

Next up was the Arizona Cardinals who were looking to draft a defensive back.

At Number. 5—Patrick Peterson to the Arizona Cardinals.

The first-round ended. Three defensive backs were taken off of the board, with Patrick Peterson at number 5, Prince Amukamara at number 19, and Jimmy Smith at number 27. The second-round observed six defensive backs to come off of the board, Ras-I Dowling at number 33, Aaron Williams at number 34, Rahim Moore at number 45, Marcus Gilchrist at number 50, Jaiquawn Jarrett at number 54, and Brandon Harris at number 60. The late first-round to early second-round projection did not come to fruition.

In the seven-rounds, two hundred and fifty-four players were selected in total. Among the defensive backs, 39 cornerbacks and 14 safeties were selected. The last pick, who the NFL refers to as Mr. Irrelevant, was outside linebacker Cheta Ozougwu to the Houston Texans. Of the 254 names called, the name "Deunta Williams" was not said.

On the first day, which is the first-round only, my name was not called. I was disappointed, but I still had hope. A lot of questions were swirling through my mind. The questions I was most fixated on were, "Why didn't you leave after your junior year?" "Was coming back to UNC worth it?" I loved my brothers-in-arms. One of my brothers, Robert Quinn, got drafted in the first-round at number 14. I was excited for his family and him. I sent him a congratulations text.

On the second day, which are the second and third-rounds, again, my name was not called. I was bewildered, but I still had hope. I was certain that I would be drafted on day number two because of all the hard work and effort put into the process. At the combine, I was masterful in the defensive back meetings and answered all of the defensive scheme-related questions exceptionally well.

Once more, teammates of mine were drafted and I was truly happy for them. In the moment, I remembered us all sitting around during the off-seasons and talking about being drafted. When I heard the names of my brothers being called, I was very happy for each of them but still longing for my name to be called.

On the third day and remaining rounds (4–7), again, my name was not called. I lost hope. Frustration began to set in. From being considered a first-round draft pick to not even being picked as Mr. Irrelevant was a deeply humbling experience.

In the back of my mind, I knew the phone call before the draft from Eugene set the stage for realism. I dialed him up in despair and frustration and decided to come clean about my irresponsible financial decisions. Fortunately, he was able to work it out with the dealership and I was able to take the SUV back. The road trip down Hwy 24 to Hwy 40 East from Jacksonville, NC to Chapel Hill, NC was a very long and reflective ride. In hindsight, giving the SUV back to the dealership was probably one of the most embarrassing incidents I have ever had to go through.

It was a bitter moment of defeat.

All of this led me to reflect on the idea of not playing in the NFL. Reflection gave way to sadness. I asked myself the following: "Was the dream being deferred?" What happens to a dream deferred? In the NFL, where the average playing career is only two and a half years, in general, and I was having a difficult time recovering from the broken leg,[7] frustration turned into depression. I was reaching a breaking point about the future direction of my life. In the midst of still recovering from a gruesome injury and hoping that at least one team would still sign me as a free agent, the dream of escaping from the impoverishment of my upbringing, creating a financially secure future for my family, and making the town of Jacksonville, NC gleam with joy because one of their own had made it; life seemed bleak. I was gifted athletically. Football had always been my big ticket out of the hood. What would I do without football? The answer would come later.

During the rehabilitation period, I tried my absolute best to not show a chink in my armor. Meaning, I did not want those around me to actually be able to see my pain and distress. Yet, these emotions grew stronger when I would run into people and they would share their stories about watching the Music City Bowl when I broke my leg. They would express how "sorry" they were for me and "wished" me well. Every one of those past conversations now seem so fuzzy to me. I would automatically respond to them with "I'll be OK" or "Things will work out fine."

After a disappointing effort to make it to the NFL following three surgeries and two medical procedures, I was declared "medically unable" to return to football. It was in this moment that I reached the climax of my breaking point. A breaking point is defined as "the moment of greatest strain at which someone or something gives way."[8] We all have a breaking point; this is a place where immense pressure has brought us to the mental, physical, or emotional edge of our composure. Within this breaking point, we are most susceptible to allowing adversity to derail us from achieving our goals. Adversity seems to strike when we least expect it and when it hits the true testament of our character is shown.

The beginning of my breaking point happened after the NCAA

suspended me at the beginning of my senior year, continued while breaking my leg on national TV during the Music City Bowl, and peaked when I did not get drafted. The NCAA broke my spirits, and it was followed by a literal break of my lower right leg. But without question, it was being undrafted by the NFL that ultimately broke my heart.

★ ★ ★

Right before the draft in a 2011 interview, I was asked, "What do you think your draft day experience will be like?" I replied:

> I think it will be a good experience. I'm not really nervous. I just want to know exactly where I'm going to be living at. Find out about my financial situation, and go on from there. I'm looking forward to working hard and seeing how I can help whatever team drafts me.[9]

In the same interview, I was asked, "If you weren't playing in the NFL, what would you want to do?" I responded:

> I think it'd [sic] [do] something involving kids and sports back in my hometown. That's definitely something that I want to do after I get done playing. I remember days when I was growing up playing in the rec league, and I couldn't get to my practices so I couldn't go to practice. But, my coaches came and picked me up, things of that nature, so that I could play. Waiving the fee and stuff like that, and all types of things, I want to make sure that kids get the same opportunities that I did.[10]

The answer to both of these questions was the heads and tails of my life. The probability of having to change my life course and do anything besides playing football seemed unlikely. However, what I, along with others aspiring to go to the NFL, often forget is that life seldom works out the way in which we plan it. As much as I visualized being the MVP of the Music City Bowl, I never visualized getting hurt and having my life to be turned upside down in the matter of moments. The attempted breakthrough from NCAA college football player to NFL football player is frequently filled with a myriad of disappointments—and in all actuality some endure worse injuries than I suffered like Rutgers player, Eric LeGrand, who was paralyzed after making a tackle against Army in the 2010 season.

To add to my disappointment, shortly after the 2011 draft, a friend sent me a link to a blog post titled, *Anyone know what happened to Deunta Williams?* One of the bloggers wrote:

> Free safety from UNC, at the start of senior season some people had him ranked as the 2nd or 3rd best safety and going around the 3rd round in the draft. He was football smart and a great ballhawking [sic] safety and yet at some point he completely disappeared [sic]. He went from this top 3 safety going in the first half of the draft, to undrafted and still unsigned safety.[11]

In early 2012 while searching the Internet, I came across a comment from a Dallas Cowboy fan who wrote, "Deunta Williams, went undrafted cause he blew out his knee in the bowl game he played in, hasn't been on a team and i [sic] really haven't heard of him [since]. He was considered to be a 1st. round if not for the injury."[12] Reading these comments on the Internet was very difficult to deal with, and personally, led to a life assessment overhaul for me.

I did my best to try to stay away from the Internet, social media, and chat rooms during this time. Up to that point, I had rehabbed my leg at UNC for almost a whole year. Being declared "medically unable" to play again was daunting enough, and I certainly did not need to compound it with the hearsay about Deunta Williams. The agony continued because teams were still calling me up to four years later after the injury. NFL teams, Canadian teams, and even Arena football teams were inquiring about my services. Each time a team would call, I had to confess that

I was "medically unable" to play football. This was a tough statement to mumble aloud to teams each and every time. In my mind, I was still hanging onto my days of glory. In the end, I had to capitulate and admit to myself that I could no longer compete anymore.

On December 30, 2010, I did not only break my lower right leg, my ego was broken as well. I felt like I lost my identity as a human being. By far the toughest part to deal with was no longer hearing the roar of the crowd. The glory received from hearing 60,000 roaring fans is an addictive feeling. The problem was that after I broke my leg, I was still addicted to that feeling. Many athletes miss "The Noise" that reverberates from the roar of the crowd when they retire by choice and/or by circumstances beyond their control. I had trouble adjusting to "The Silence."

It was only through God's glory and grace that an old but refined dream emerged to change my perspective on life. Thinking back to the 2011 interview when I was asked, "If you weren't playing in the NFL, what would you want to do?" I responded, "I think it'd [do] something involving kids and sports back in my hometown."[13] Dedicating my life to the kids (and adults) of Jacksonville is exactly what I did to make a positive difference in the community.

First, I graduated from UNC with a Bachelors degree in Management and Society[14], and then went on to obtain my Masters of Business Administration (MBA) from the Keller Graduate School of Management at DeVry University. I was on my way back to reclaiming my "champion mindset." I transferred the work ethic from the football field to the world of entrepreneurship and became an investor in corporate and residential real estate, corporate stocks and bonds, and even a mobile app. Second, in 2012, to keep my promise to the kids of Jacksonville, I developed a 501c-3 non-profit, E.M.E.R.G.E. (Empowering Messages, Expanding Resources, Genuine Engagement), to increase youth achievement and eliminate the achievement gaps that exist throughout our educational system. In this role, I am doing more than facilitating sporting activities for kids, I am molding the leaders of tomorrow in Jacksonville, NC and around the global world. I did not want to live and die and do nothing for the community who gave so much to me. I wanted to do my part.

E.M.E.R.G.E. gave me this opportunity.

Our former First Lady of the United States, Eleanor Roosevelt once said, "With the new day comes new strength and new thoughts." When my breaking point came, I was faced with a lot of questions related to my identity: How do I transition from shelving the helmet, shoulder pads, and cleats to a life away from football? How do I gain the strength to move on from football? What new thoughts will consume me after football? These three reflective questions all end with one word: "football." This is because football was my life.

I wrote this book to show others how to heal after their breaking point—whether it be in the world of sports or life in general. In order to heal, you must be resilient. Throughout my life, I have learned that being resilient is the name of the game, and in fact, the only viable response to adversity. We all go through a point in our lives where a hard decision has to be made and often requires a life assessment overhaul. Luckily, for me, my breaking point came earlier than most. Many athletes who actually make it to the NFL or other forms of professional sports not only suffer from lasting injuries and trauma, but also, financial hardship and an identity crisis after they retire. Most pressing today, current and retired NFL athletes suffer concussions, which often times lead to dementia, Alzheimer's disease, and chronic traumatic encephalopathy (CTE). Sadly, these are the realities of the profession.

In this light, I chose to view my breaking point as something positive and practice acceptance of a new direction for my life. It is down this path where I realized that my life was bigger than football. I share with you my story. It is one of resilience and rebirth after my breaking point.

CHAPTER 2
ADVERSITY: THE ROAD TO NEVERLAND

Proverbs 3:4–6 reads, "4 Then you will win favor and a good name in the sight of God and man. 5 Trust in the LORD with all your heart and lean not on your own understanding; 6 in all your ways submit to him, and he will make your paths straight."

The imagination frames adversity in ways unimaginable—- usually good, bad, and ugly. Through these different frames of life there is normally a silver lining that provides hope. The elusive term, "hope," was the foundation of my upbringing.

I hoped my Nana, who is the rock of our family, would live to see her grandson become a man.

I hoped God would ease the burden on my mother. I watched how hard she worked to provide for our family. She instilled in me a strong work ethic.

I hoped my family could escape poverty and move out of the projects one day. Quite frankly, living in poverty sucked. You can easily develop a hopeless mindset early on in life because of the circumstances you are handed at birth. You do not get to pick if you are black or white, if you are tall or short, or even if you are rich or poor. The only thing you can do as a kid is try to develop the will power to determine how your future is going to be! And as a kid, I wanted to achieve the big American Dream and everything that came with it.

I hoped a poor project kid from Jacksonville, NC could discover a "talent" to elevate my family from poverty status. I wanted to figure out my talent in order to help those most influential in my life—- my grandmother, my mother, and my uncle—-who, all together, were my strongest support system and pivotal in helping me develop from a young boy into a grown man. In addition, I wanted to make the supportive web of principals, teachers, coaches, church congregations, other athletes in the city, and friends proud of me.

I never wanted the glimmer of hope to fade and place me on the Road to Neverland. What is the Road to Neverland? It is a path paved with endless adversity, hardship, suffering, and trials and tribulations. Along this path, adversity can define us and we never get to experience the ever-flowing fruits of good fortune. It is difficult to have a healthy quality of life and easy to make poor life decisions. This path is not a desired course, yet some of us are born into this space— kids born in the ghetto, kids born with inherited trials and tribulations.

I know we are to accept that life's trials and tribulations help to develop character and empower us to become resilient; however, we should not have to live a life defined by our trials and tribulations. Through it all, God has shown me that life's trials and tribulations have purpose and reward. I am fortunate that from childhood to adulthood, He has diverted my path away from the Road to Neverland, allowing me to keep "hope" alive.

The Good and The Bad

At the center of my life is my Nana, Doretha Jane Williams. She is the backbone of our family. To say that she is the most influential person in my life would be an understatement. My Nana is the glue that has kept all of the family bonded. What I have learned from her is that "family" and "love" work in universal harmony. Her life's code is, "Love one another; as I have loved you. So you must love one another" (John 13:34).

My Nana is 72-years-old. She and my grandfather, Dave Williams, married in 1963. They were together for 18 years before he passed away. I was only 4-years-old at the time. I do not remember a lot about my grandfather but I know that he made ends meet. The stories that have churned around are that he hustled hard to feed his family. This work ethic allowed my Nana to be a housewife before his death. After he passed away, Nana had to get a job working as a cafeteria lady.

She had a total of six children—— four boys and two girls. The two girls were twins. My mother was one of them. On January 6, 1970, my mother, Danine, was born, followed by my aunt, Janine. Since my mother gave birth to me at such a young age, my Nana basically had seven children to raise in the household. To this day, she considers me her seventh child as well as her first grandchild.

My Nana raised my aunts and uncles in the Sandy Run Projects in Jacksonville, NC. Sandy Run has a total of 152 units, 127 of which are Section 8 assisted living units. Raising her children in the projects was an emotional challenge, but it was one that my Nana faced head-on. There were years of overcoming considerable obstacles. With a family to feed and take care of on limited resources, my Nana created a loving environment for the whole family; the love filled in the gaps left from having little to nothing.

There is a reason that this time of my life was good and bad. I am reminded of so many moments from all of the family sitting around during the holidays. We were too poor to travel, so sitting around and telling stories took my mind on a journey. Family get-togethers were a special time in the Williams' household. Thanksgiving. Christmas. Easter. Fourth of July. I loved these holidays. The magic of the holiday season brought a great deal of love into our project unit when the whole family was together.

In the summers, my Nana would solicit my services to make "Hard cups." These are frozen Kool-Aid cups for the youngsters. We would make a pitcher of sugar-loaded Kool-Aid and pour it into individual five-ounce paper cups and allow it to freeze. My Nana would charge the kids in the projects 50 cents for a cup. She was the owner of *Ms. Doretha's Hard Cups* and I was her best employee, even though I ate more cups than I helped her sell.

My Nana has lived a very fortunate life in the sense that she has preached love and every one gave her love in return. She has always said, "Family is all that we got." The good fortune of watching my Nana as a case study for hard work is that because of her diligence to give us a better life, all of her children were eventually able to either move out of the projects and into houses, decent apartment complexes, or better Section 8 assisted living places. At one time my entire family lived in the Sandy Run Projects and slowly but surely we all were able to make it out. Those good times and bad times taught me that, "Family is all that we got."

Perhaps the greatest thing my Nana gave me was the ability to see life with rare objectivity. I watched as she faced life's trials and tribulations head-on. We know that most people are not objective-driven human beings. My Nana, however, is one of the few people who chooses to see people through a lens that almost eliminates bias and prejudice. She taught me never to judge. She taught me that family should do for one another. She taught me humility. Her keen objectivity taught me to be humble. As I often describe her, my Nana is my peace.

In high school I made a promise to my Nana that when I was drafted into the NFL, I would buy her a home. I wanted to reward her for the sacrifices she made for our family. The plan was to buy her a home and help her to retire. Watching her struggle to raise all of us was great motivation. When I broke my leg during the bowl game, I worried how I could fulfill that promise. Through the grace of God, I was still able to bring that promise to fruition with the monies from an insurance policy obtained in college in the event of a career-ending football injury. After I was declared medically unable to return to football, the monies paid out. It was a very proud moment when I placed the keys to her own house in her hands.

★ ★ ★

My mother, Danine Dale Collins, is a shining light of love. When I was a child, her hugs and kisses as forms of affection would fill my heart with much joy. Little boys tend to gravitate to their mothers to be coddled. From a young age, we are taught to love and take care of our mothers. We usually end up being "momma's boys." Since my mother had me at such a young age, I never turned into a "momma's boy." I was a "grandma's boy." My Nana provided a nurturing type of love that my mother could not in the beginning.

I spent a lot of my time with my Nana while my mother was at work providing for our family. I relied on her, and she relied on me. This matriarchal transfer of responsibility is commonplace within the black community. As a result, a great number of black children become "grandma's boy" and "grandma's girl," identifying with the primary caregiver.

My mother was 17-years-old when she had me— young, black, living in poverty, and raising me without my father. These are considered classic structural and cultural elements of the detriment of teenage pregnancies within the black community that often continues generational poverty and limited access to valuable resources. From generation to generation within the black community, babies raising babies and fatherless sons and daughters have become the norm in a lot of ways.

We were fortunate to move out of the projects when I was 8-years-old and into better Section 8 assisted living places. The term *better* is operative. We lived in run-down apartments and even lived in a mobile home at one point. Lots of time was spent moving in and out of apartments, section-8 rentals, and at times having to move in with my Nana at her house. Before the 7th grade we had moved around about ten different times, even moving to Texas and back to Jacksonville. I attended two different elementary schools and three different middle schools. There was no home stability growing up but the love my mother bestowed was always constant.

Mothers in single-parent endeavors, like my mother, often have to make the ultimate sacrifice for their children and sometimes have to either drop out of high school or forgo college. Their education comes from real life experiences. Their instruction comes in the form of eviction notices and the renting of U-Haul trucks due to constant moving around. Their grade comes from making sure that ends meet. A grade of "F" can lead to homelessness.

Two years after I was born, my mother gave birth to my younger brother, Adrain Williams. His birth also accelerated my growth. It placed more responsibility on me in my childhood years. As in most single-parent households, the eldest child has to grow up fast. I had to balance being a kid while also being a role model to my younger brother. I actually relished this responsibility. I took great pleasure in being a role model for him. I love my little brother.

My mother always had two jobs and worked hard each and every day to put food on the table for my little brother and myself. There were times when we would eat while she sacrificed by not eating as much. We did not have much, but she made sure we always had two things: food on the table and a roof over our heads.

One of her favorite sayings is, "Everybody knows that I would go broke for my kids." I do not know how she did it, but my mother always provided for us. Christmas was my mother's favorite time of the year. Every Christmas, she would work a miracle. We always had enough gifts to make us feel like it was really Christmas.

Even still, I was one of those kids who did not ask for much growing up. Partly because I came to realize that we did not have the financial means for extras. Despite understanding this, my mother never harped on our financial condition. She never said, "We are broke, baby" or "We are on welfare, baby." She may have said at most, "Mama can't afford that right now." No unnecessary attention was drawn to our financial condition. It may be difficult to control your circumstances, but you can control your mindset. She did a good job of raising us to believe in this concept. My mother would say every blue moon, "Yeah, we may live in poverty, but we don't have to be of poverty." She never discussed impoverishment in a way that made us feel sorry for ourselves.

One time my mother told me that she only made $18,000 a year. I had to have been around 14-years-old or so during this time. To make extra money, she would clean commercial properties for under-the-table profit. That was the money she did not report to the IRS. She hustled tirelessly to cope with the status of our economic condition as we hovered around the poverty line.

During my teenage years, I began to see the clear differences between those who have and those who do not have. It is hard not to look at others that have and wish that you had a little more too. When I would visit my friends, I would always look at the cereal they had at their house. They had Fruit Loops, Captain Crunch, Lucky Charms, Cookie Crisp, and Frosted Flakes while we had generic cereal or none at all. The only time I would try those types of cereal would be at their house because certain welfare benefits only allowed you to have Corn Flakes or Chex. Foods like Vienna sausages, Treet meat, Spam, Potted meat, and Ramen Noodles were the dishes we were most accustom to. We also feasted on toast with syrup, honey buns, pecan spinwheels sweet rolls, and ice cream sandwiches. These are all poor-related delicacies in the hood.

The most righteous thing about the story of growing up in an impoverished, single-parent household is the will to survive; no matter what we did or did not have, we survived. My mother made sure of that! Poverty did not stop her. Teenage pregnancy did not stop her. Raising me without a father did not stop her. Nothing stopped her from doing her absolute best to provide a healthy quality of life for our family. My mother did her best to eliminate the stigma of unwed black mothers who make their circumstances harder. Over the years, I watched how hard she worked and took my cues from her and my Nana about the consequential value of having a strong work ethic.

My mother could write a best seller about the exploits of a black single-mother raising two black sons. She lived it. Both of her children made it out of the hood. Both attended and graduated from college. Both are now productive citizens. The lady who "would go broke for her children" contributed to breaking the cycle of young black males born into single-parent households that either end up in prison or the grave. Round of applause, Mama Danine!

The Ugly

My mother had to learn to be my mother and my father. Children born into "fatherless" homes are often presented with challenges that affect their growth and development. We know it is absolutely important, but not mandatory, that a child is surrounded by the love of both parents for the betterment of their own well-being.

Fortunately for me, I did have positive male role models. They were my three uncles—Henry, Lamont, and Chris. They provided a great deal of love and support. My uncles acted as a collective of surrogate fathers in the absence of my biological father.

There was no biological father in my life until my teenage years. Unfortunately, the sad reality is that my mother did not acknowledge my father. Nor did I ever inquire about having a father. It may sound strange to most but I never asked her about my father. I just assumed that he did not want anything to do with me. If he did not want anything to do with me, then I did not want anything to do with him.

In my childhood, not knowing my father privately affected me emotionally and mentally for quite some time. My mother is a wonderful woman but she could not truly teach me about becoming a man. I can honestly say that not having a father in my early years was probably the biggest void in my life. It left a gap in my soul. Most kids that grow up without a father never understand the ripple effect that it has on their lives. I was the same. There was no father to teach me how to ride a bike. There was no father to teach me how to catch a baseball. There was no father to teach me how to throw a football. More importantly, there was no father to teach me how to handle life's trials and tribulations. There was no affirming that only a father can give to his son.

When I saw nuclear families—father, mother, and children— together it was strange to me. It was like a slap in the face seeing "true" family interaction. As much as my Nana, my mother, and my uncles were a great base, I never got to experience what life would have been like if I could have woken up in the morning and seen my father and my mother in the kitchen making breakfast, letting me help, and then us all sitting down as a family to eat. This is a simple, yet powerful, visual that is lost in a single-parent household.

I never got a chance to understand the positive dynamics of having two parents in the home and the value that a father brings to a household. The reason this sucks is because what I have come to learn is that a man brings a masculine firmness and strength to a family. For me, a sense of guidance was missing from my childhood without a father and it led to internal issues that affected my self- confidence and self-worth.

* * *

I learned the identity of my biological father in my teenage years. Up until the age of 15, I was under the impression that I did not have an active father by his choice. Like I said, if he did not want anything to do with me, then I did not want anything to do with him. If I was ever asked about having a father, I would tell people that I did not have one. This abnormal statement seemed normal in my world. Of course the person in the conversation would attempt to challenge this premise and indicate that it was biologically and physically impossible not to have a father. For the first 14 years of my life, I simply did not have a father present. Thus, in my mind, I did not have one.

At the age of 15, I was hit with a bombshell. My mother had been holding onto an explosive and dark secret. By process of elimination, she had known exactly who my biological father was since I was 4-years-old. She held onto this secret because of the circumstances surrounding her pregnancy. Disclosing the identity of my father could have led to the termination of his employment and disrupted his family situation.

Back in the day my mother was a high school track and field star—including trophies, medals, and ribbons. She even held a few state records that have stood the test of time. My mother found out she was pregnant in her fifth month. I became more active in the womb which led to her running slower times. When she found out, my mother had to quit the track team immediately.

During this time, my mother had a boyfriend. So for the longest, they thought he was my biological father. His family and friends were in his ear leading him to question whether he was my biological father or not. I was much darker than him and did not strike a strong resemblance. Later I would take a paternity test that proved he was not my biological father. Feelings were hurt, and rightfully so. All ties were severed.

After the paternity test, my mother knew who my biological father was. She may have known before that, but held the secret close to her.

This time, she held onto the secret even tighter. This could potentially impact the lives of many people. Therefore, to protect all those involved, which consequently affected me, she held onto the secret.

When I was 15-years-old, the secret came out in the most shocking way. To qualify for Medicaid, my mother had to show that she knew my biological father. After the test, the truth was revealed. The identity of my biological father was my mother's former high school track coach.

One day after the paternity test, my mother called me to her room. She asked me to close the door behind me and took my hands. We then said a prayer. I am not going to lie; I initially thought that I was in serious trouble. When a black mother closes the door, and then says a prayer, usually an extension-cord-beating is to follow. My mind was racing thinking about all of the possibilities of what I had done wrong.

As my mother began to speak, I could see that there was something much deeper emerging from our conversation. Her posture was different. Her tone was different. And the words coming out of her mouth would be unlike any I had heard before. We talked for about 30-minutes although it felt as if I had been in her room for hours. The whole conversation seemed to be in slow motion. I was totally caught off guard and at a loss for words.

My mother apologized for keeping this secret from me. I gave her a hug and told her things would be all right. I also thanked her for telling me the truth. Before she called me to her room, I was practicing my saxophone. To process our conversation, I returned back to playing my saxophone to make sense of things in my mind. I wondered, would inserting my father into our lives serve us well? The more I processed, the better I played the saxophone. I wish I could have recorded that practice session because the notes were flowing out of me. It felt like it was the very first time I was able to play freely, as if I was expressing my thoughts and emotions through my horn. The feeling was liberating to say the least. I will never forget that night.

I woke up the next day feeling more connected to the world. I showed up to school about 30 minutes earlier than usual to get breakfast. I was anxiously awaiting the arrival of my best friend to tell him the news that he was actually my brother as well! As we were finishing our breakfast, I pulled him to the side. I asked if he had talked to his pops. He said, "No, what's up?" Then, I just told him, "Yo dude, we are brothers." He originally laughed it off because I always kept a good joke going. Plus, for some reason, I had mastered the art of giving serious news with a smile on my face.

Throughout the rest of the school day, I kept trying to tell him that I was not playing. I told him over and over again, "Dude, we are brothers. Like real brothers. No Bull****." The whole day was a blur but later that night he called me and told me that his father, and mine too now, told him that we are, in fact, real brothers. I know the information was a ton for him to process as well. And for the record, finding out that my best friend is actually my brother was pretty cool. We had been close friends for many years. The next day I saw him. We both agreed that the news would only bring us closer.

Later, I found out that I actually had an additional four siblings. In a matter of days, I learned the name of my father and that I had two older brothers and two younger sisters. It took me a while to come to terms with the full situation, but it was and continues to be, wonderful to have all of them in my life. Like many brothers and sisters, we are a family now. The way it took place could not tarnish that.

My father was the one to make the next move. About a week later when picking up my brother from school, my father pulled me to the side and we talked briefly. The conversation started with "Hello Deunta, I am your father" and ended with him inviting me to shoot hoops with him later that day. This was his way of attempting to bond.

Before arriving to shoot hoops with my father, many emotional thoughts came over me. To be honest, I did not know how to even greet him, what to say, or how to feel. How should I react to a man who was not a part of my life for the first 14 years? Did he ever see me in public and think that I could be his son? My emotions were all over the place. Rightfully so in this moment; I was about to formally meet, and have a lengthy talk, with my biological father for the first time and on the basketball court of all places.

We met. We talked. We shot hoops. We bonded. After shooting hoops, we talked for hours. Any and every question that I asked, he answered freely and openly. I wanted him to acknowledge me as his son. A father is a son's first hero. My hero had been M.I.A. for a long time. But now, he was finally in my life.

On the ride home, we stopped and got some ice cream from Dairy Queen. I kept looking at him, and then looking at myself in the mirror. I guess I was still in disbelief. Looking at my father's face was like looking at an older version of myself. It became undeniable, he was my father and I was his son!

* * *

As you could imagine, finding out about new family members took a toll on both sides of my family but it never got too ugly. Between my father's side and my mother's side cooler heads prevailed. Both families accepted the news with grace. Potential fights were avoided among the adults to ensure that the children got to know each other.

Personally, it was very tough for me to be caught in the middle of my parent's sins from their past. For years, there was an awkwardness about the whole situation. It took until my senior year in college before we could all be in the same place without the air being sucked out of the room. My entire family was able to wrap me up in love and support. Through that love and support, I was able to reckon with this difficult time.

I was excited about the idea of having a father. But then again, I did not want to rake my mother over the coals for holding onto this secret. He made a mistake and she made a mistake. Those two mistakes led to my conception. I am thankful for that.

At the end of the day, I did not ask to be here. An ugly situation eventually led to a beautiful outcome. Finding my father moved my life forward. On one hand, I could have hated him for all of the time he missed. On the other hand, I could find a sense of peace and genuine love for him. I chose the latter. Ever since I forged a bond with my father, my heart has been on the future and not the past.

The Silver Lining of My Life

Through the good times, bad times, and ugly times, there was one silver lining that helped my life to reach a perfect balance: Football.

Football was my solace. The activity of playing football grounded me in a mental and physical space I had never experienced before in my life. Playing football gave me freedom from life's trials and tribulations. Football diverted my path from the Road to Neverland.

I was eight-years-old the first time I played organized football for the recreation league. In my very first game, the head coach placed me on the field to return kickoffs. Neither one of us thought the kicker would kick it far enough for me to receive the football. I remember watching the ball floating in the air towards me. All I could think was, "Please lord, just let me catch this ball." On that day, the football Gods decided to call my number. I caught the ball and began to zig and zag across the football field. I was running scared trying not to get hit. Sixty yards later, the end product of my mad dash was six points on the scoreboard. Touchdown!

It was my Uncle Henry who told me at the end of my 8th grade year that if I worked hard for the next four years of my life, I, Deunta Williams, a poor kid from the projects, could earn, through sports, a college scholarship. His words were inspirational. My uncle made me believe that what I wanted existed and was mine for the taking. Although, he warned me that it would not be easy. Only through hard work, dedication, and sacrifice, would I achieve the goal. His talk widened my perspective. I had "poor-tential" and my uncle knew that. The prefix of "poor" was the motivation to work my butt off and provide a better life for my family and myself.

My Uncle Henry really planted a seed of hope. Through our conversation, I made a solemn promise to him and football. The seed grew inside me, and I turned most of my actions into making this a reality. I committed myself to football—-not only in words, but also in action. Every day I focused on getting better. I worked out hard. I practiced hard. I played hard. I did not want to cheat football and I did not want it to cheat me. Football had become my official ticket out of the hood.

I was obsessed with the idea of using football to obtain a college scholarship. Through football, I could block out real life and make everything about "making it." I had the ability to compartmentalize life and use various life circumstances to motivate me. When we had to move to another living space, I told myself to work harder. When my mother could not afford to buy my brother and I certain clothes and tennis shoes, I told myself to work harder. When we had to eat Vienna sausages, Treet Meat, Spam, Potted meat, and Ramen Noodles, I told myself to work harder. I had one goal and that was to "make it."

★ ★ ★

In high school, I started to make a name for myself. After spending half of my freshman season on the junior varsity football team, I was moved up to the varsity. The football Gods had intervened again. During the season, one of the varsity running backs got suspended. As a result, the varsity head coach pulled me up. I can still remember him walking into my band class to tell me I was promoted to the varsity team. Coach had a varsity jersey draped over his shoulder. He asked to speak with me outside of the room. I returned to band class with the jersey now over my shoulder. My freshmen classmates all gave me a round of applause.

On the varsity team, I was further able to prove my skills to the coaches and see immediate playing time. The head coach had enough confidence in me to start me at running back for a few playoff games. I started the season on the junior varsity to now being considered one of the best players on the entire team. It was a great start to my football career because I started turning heads and earning respect in Jacksonville.

Recognition of my athletic talents continued when I also made the varsity basketball team. There was a great difference between the two sports. In football, I was a natural. In basketball, I had to work harder to make the varsity team. I was starting on both the football and basketball teams in my freshman year of high school. After basketball season, I also decided to join the track team. Since my mother was an exceptional athlete in track and field, I wanted to continue her legacy.

I became an All-area athlete and was offered a scholarship in each of the three sports. Even as a three-sport athlete, it was clear that football would be the best route to receive a college scholarship from a top college football program. The writing was on the wall. The combination of my size, height, and athleticism were most suited to grace the gridiron. The college football field is 360 feet long and 160 feet wide. My goal was to earn a scholarship and make that space my safe haven.

Throughout my high school playing days, I posted great stats in football. I was beginning to be recognized as a top-tier athlete among college programs. I went on to make the All-area and All-state teams in football. At first, smaller schools were contacting me about playing for their programs. While I was most appreciative and did not want to overlook any school, I had my sights set on a top-ranked Division I-A football program.

When I heard college coaches were coming to a game to evaluate a current prospect and it was not me, I made sure to try to catch their attention. In my mind, I was one of the best prospects in the nation and wanted colleges to see my "poor-tential." I wanted them to know that Deunta Williams was an exceptional football player who had great character, made good grades, and would be an excellent "fit" for their program.

After my junior year, I was invited to the Rivals All-American combine. All of the biggest names involving North Carolina high school football were in attendance for the event. Even though I had pulled my hamstring in a track and field conference meet the week before, I still performed well in the drills. I was determined to make a name for myself in front of the people who could offer me a scholarship.

The defining moment for me came during the vertical jump. I set a record at 41 ½ inches. Coaches and players were surrounding me, watching me jump. Each time I would jump, I would record a higher and higher mark. Participants' usually only get three jumps, but they wanted me to go for the record. After my eighth jump, I set the national record. After the Rivals All-American combine, I was selected as a pre-season North Carolina All-American in football. This opened the eyes of a lot of top-ranked Division I-A football programs and really accelerated the recruitment process.

The recruitment process for me was a great time in my life. I was always humbled when a coach showed interest in my ability to play and help their program. I received tubs full of recruitment letters, game-day programs, and posters from all of the universities recruiting me. I had an awesome time visiting the various university campuses. Overall, the recruitment process was an invaluable experience. Growing up, I thought I had no value as a child born into poverty to now becoming a person who people valued.

Equally important, I was happy to keep the solemn promise made to my Uncle Henry. He was a part of the recruitment process. I made sure of that. My uncle was once a stud, college athlete himself. He knew the in's and out's of the process. He also knew how to feel coaches out. On one of my recruiting trips, I remember turning and asking my uncle, "Do you feel this coach?" He laughed at me because he saw how excited I was to be going through the recruitment process. His support meant the world to me.

Whenever talking to a coach during the recruitment process, I was full of excitement because I knew it put me one step closer to making my Nana, my mother, and all of my uncles proud. The first grandchild was on the verge of receiving a college scholarship. The first son born to Danine Dale Collins was on the verge of receiving a college scholarship. The little boy who returned a kick-off for a touchdown in his first orga-nized football game was on the verge of receiving a college scholarship. A college scholarship is a big deal in the black home. It can often define the trajectory of black life, and it did for me.

On February 1, 2006, I officially signed a letter of intent to play college football for the University of North Carolina. I was beyond ex-cited. My family was excited. My high school teammates were excited. It was an exciting moment in my life. I visited many universities during the recruitment process but all fell short in comparison to the beautiful and majestic atmosphere of Chapel Hill.

As a North Carolina native, I got an opportunity to play for the flagship school in the state. I was Carolina raised and Carolina proud.

Now, I was going to be attending the University of North Carolina in Chapel Hill, NC. "A Tar Heel born, a Tar Heel bred, and when I die, a Tar Heel dead!"

It was a day of celebration. Not only because I received the scholarship, but also, because through the work ethic instilled in me by loved ones, going off to college was allowing me to venture further and further away from the Road to Neverland and helping me to land on the path to promise.

I wanted it, I worked hard for it, and then I seized it.

CHAPTER 3
GROWTH: LESSONS LEARNED

1 John 2:1 reads, "My dear children, I write this to you so that you will not sin. But if anybody does sin, we have an advocate with the Father, Jesus Christ, the Righteous One."

One of the most crucial lessons to learn in life is how to mature and grow from life's trials and tribulations. Between the ages of 15 and 18-years-old, my life was in a whirlwind. From this whirlwind, a great opportunity was presented to play college football. It opened my life to a brave new world.

In the summer of 2006, I embarked upon a new journey from Jacksonville, NC to Chapel Hill, NC. The transition from Deunta Williams, three-sport star athlete, born and raised in Jacksonville, to incoming freshman, unproven, in Chapel Hill, was exciting and thrilling, yet daunting and intimidating. There were quite a few thoughts that consumed my mind during this transitional period. First and foremost, I wanted to fulfill my solemn promise to my uncle. Second, I wanted be a good student-athlete who went to class and made good grades. I had experienced academic success throughout my upbringing so I was thrilled at the opportunity to further challenge my mind. Third, I wanted to complete my college degree to make my Nana and my mother proud. Last and most importantly, I wanted to prove to myself that I could compete with the very best athletes across the country and eventually make it to "The League."

My time spent at UNC would be wonderful but challenging. It was a beautiful time in my life filled with a lot of growth, hard work, sacrifice, good times, bad times, and mistakes made. Throughout this time, a lot of lessons were learned. In the process of finding a way to balance being a black male student-athlete at a predominantly white institution (PWI) and performing at a high level on the gridiron, my world was turned upside down when the NCAA suspended me at the height of my college football career.

After deciding to return for my senior year instead of entering the NFL draft, allegations swirled that I received $1,426 in "improper benefits" leading to a four game suspension. The NCAA said my suspension was based on "preferential treatment." Subsequently, this investigation by the NCAA into "improper benefits" to football players also led to the uncovering of academic misconduct at UNC that started in 1993 and ended in 2011. Unbeknownst to the general public at the time, many student-athletes, including myself, willingly but not maliciously participated in an academic fraud scheme to remain academically eligible and/or to take a course with less academic demands than traditional lecture courses. On and off of the football field, both scandals were a major distraction in my life. Each scandal would eventually cast a dark cloud over my name.

At the pinnacle of my college life and football career, I was standing out from the crowd for the wrong reasons. The funny thing is, before I left for UNC as a freshman, my Nana said to me, "Good decisions lead to a good life." The kid from the Sandy Run Projects in Jacksonville, NC whose Nana, mother, and uncle had worked their tails off to make sure he did veer away from the Road to Neverland, was now praying day and night and night and day that his poor decisions would not derail his promising future and lead all those who believed in him to now question his character.

This chapter is as transparent as possible about my time at UNC because where facts ends, speculation begins, and there is no truth. During this time in my life, I knew that persevering through the NCAA suspension and allegations of academic misconduct would set the stage for my big comeback. In order to move forward, I would need to make the best decisions possible to stay the course on the path to promise.

Being an NCAA Student-Athlete

Stepping onto the campus of UNC was like walking into a brave new world given my humble beginnings. Who goes to UNC? According to the website, "Students ready to challenge themselves with talented classmates and top-notch professors on one residential campus in the ultimate college town."[15]

UNC continues to be an institution that houses top-notch professors settled inside of an ultimate college town. I really enjoyed my time at UNC. I had some amazing professors; even still to this day, I can call up my Economics or Sports and Exercise professors to chat about life. It truly is a great university that offers a quality education. I have always been a big advocate of education. I am of the belief that people's lives can be transformed through the power of education.

Equally important, being in the university and college setting helps to develop social skills and teaches students how to become responsible adults. One of the best things about going to UNC was the chance to meet a diverse group of talented students at the university. My experiences on campus definitely broadened my horizons.

Once you add the term "athlete" to the equation, the experience in college can be framed in a different light. To begin, student-athletes are held to a higher standard of student conduct. For example, each student-athlete recruited to a university is a representative of their families, communities, and themselves. It would be a great disservice to the maturation of the said student-athlete to lower those standards. Student-athletes hold a great responsibility. With such responsibility, comes great accountability.

Similarly, universities coming to recruit student-athletes hold a great responsibility as well. The university has a responsibility first to that student-athlete, and second to the environment that the student-athlete comes from. Student-athletes are recruited from across diverse demographics and backgrounds. Because of this, the university should have cultural competency measures and staff in place. That is, an organization or group of people who possess relatable attitudes and behaviors to the student-athletes, especially the black student-athletes.

As a student-athlete, my experience at UNC was different than that of the traditional student. I was expected to be a high-performance athlete signed to a contractual scholarship to help the football program win games. Two words that can describe some of my first moments being a NCAA Division I student-athlete were: "Culture Shock." I can remember the first workout like it was yesterday. The coaches worked us hard enough that some of us considered quitting. It was evident that they wanted to sift out the very best athletes. The coaches wanted to see which players were going to quit. The workouts were designed to separate the weak from the strong. It was the price we, as football players at a top-notch football program, had to pay to keep our scholarships.

I worked hard all summer in the hopes I could earn the chance to play in my true freshman year (i.e., first year out of high school). When I reported for training camp in August, the nervousness that flutters within the heat of competition filled our practice site. We had some notable freshmen athletes in the 2006 recruiting class. The veteran players were ready to compete to retain their starting positions and the freshmen were adamant about earning a starting roster spot. This was the glory of competition.

Unfortunately, fate intervened and denied me the ability to even compete for a starting roster spot as a true freshman. I developed a bad case of patellar tendonitis on the second day of training camp. I assumed it was related to the triple jump competitions in track and field during my senior year in high school. I worked with the medical staff every day to speed the healing process but I was not symptom-free until the season was nearly over. As a result, I was redshirted my first year.

Redshirting actually turned out to be a blessing in disguise. I needed the extra year to work on my study habits and get off to a good start academically. Adjusting to the academic demands at UNC was also a "Culture Shock." It was a different academic standard than high school. Although I had graduated from high school with a high GPA, I soon learned college courses had a much higher demand. This was new territory for me. Nonetheless, I finished my freshman year with a GPA above 3.0 and received an academic award for that accomplishment.

As much as I loved learning, football was always my #1 priority. For most student-athletes, our student designation on campus is ambiguous. The term "student-athlete" implies that equal time is spent in our respective sport and toward our academics; yet, during the football season, we often spent more time doing football-related activities than attending academic-related learning sessions. In my opinion, the modification of this ambiguous term, "student-athlete," is critical. At a top-notch Division I-A football program, it should be modified to "athlete-student" to accurately reflect the football-related demands for incoming freshman and all students involved in athletics.

We all know that the emphasis is on winning. If the emphasis were truly on academics, coaches would not get fired. If the emphasis were truly on academics, athletic training schedules would facilitate more time for academics. If the emphasis were truly on academics, all scholarships would be guaranteed for four years or until a student graduated from college. There are no "full" scholarships, only year-to-year contracts. Living and breathing in this win-at-all-cost environment shaped and conditioned my perspective about football. I was being primed to adhere to the culture within the "Big Business of College Athletics," in which a dominant winning mentality passes down from generation to generation.

* * *

The next year, I came back bigger, stronger, and faster after a gruesome commitment to our off-season strength and conditioning program. I was amazed at how much I developed physically in one year; hard work paid off. I was named the ACC Defensive Rookie of the Year, First-Team All-ACC Freshman team, and received Freshman All-American honors. I was very grateful to win all of these personal accolades, especially in my first year of actually playing at UNC. My coaches, teammates, and entire support system were paramount in winning these awards. From my true freshman year to my redshirt freshman year, I worked harder than I had ever worked in my life to improve as a football player and it showed on the field.

Back home my Nana, my mother, my uncles, and my hometown of Jacksonville was extremely proud of me. My accomplishments were their accomplishments. I remember all of the love I received from them via phones calls, text messages, Facebook, and even a front-page story on the sports page in the *Jacksonville Daily News.* My accomplishments were bigger than me. All I wanted to do was make the people of Jacksonville proud.

After such a breakout year, my life was changing rapidly. Can you imagine being one of the star players on a major NCAA Division I-A football team? For me, it was a great time to be alive. It was hard to wrap my mind around. People on campus and around town began to see me differently. They viewed me as a player who could possibly make it to the NFL. Students began to ask for my autograph on campus and asked me to sign items as souvenirs. It truly was a surreal experience.

The success continued throughout my redshirt sophomore (2008 season) and redshirt junior (2009 season) years. In my redshirt sophomore year, I recorded 65 total tackles and had three interceptions. The following year, I recorded 47 total tackles and had six interceptions. For the 2009 season, I was named First-Team All-ACC.

At this point, NFL scouts were beginning to inquire about me. I was slowly moving onto the NFL big board, which forecasts the top college prospects in the upcoming year. The combination of my size, strength, and athleticism was appealing to scouts. The bold existence of professional football stardom seemed to be upon me, and I was excited to capitalize off of this awesome moment in my life.

Life Comes at You Fast:
The NCAA Scandal

On May 29, 2010, writing from a hotel room in Miami at 6:07 a.m.,[16] my former teammate, Marvin Austin, tweeted, "I live In club LIV so I get the tenant rate. bottles comin [*sic*] like its giveaway."[17] Austin was the star defensive tackle on our team. His tweet was heard around the college football world and led the NCAA to spark an investigation into him and the UNC football program.

The NCAA found that Austin had been given nearly $24,000 in cash, airline tickets, and received paid hotel rooms from former sports agent, Terry Watson. They launched an investigation first into Austin and his social media, and then into other UNC players' public and private accounts. The NCAA demanded access to the players phone records and private text messages. The investigation initially centered around "improper benefits" and "improper contact" with sports agents but would eventually reveal academic misconduct.

Then-UNC players Robert Quinn and Greg Little were also said to receive improper benefits from Watson. It was alleged that all three players lied about receiving improper benefits. They were suspended for the entire 2010 season and eventually received "permanent disassociation" letters on November 15, 2013. Austin, Quinn, and Little—my brothers-in-arms— received a lifetime ban from Kenan Memorial Stadium and all athletic facilities on the campus in addition to being prohibited from any association and contact with any current athletes at UNC.

Before the 2010 season began, 18 football players in total were implicated in the investigation and placed on suspension amid the NCAA investigation. During the season opener against Louisiana State University (LSU), 13 players were officially suspended. I was one of those 13 players. We would find out later that six of our players were suspended for the season. It hurt so bad to not be on the field with my brothers-in-arms that I did not even go to the stadium for our season opener. I watched the game at my apartment with family. I was damn near in tears!

Pertaining to my case, the NCAA alleged that I received "improper benefits." During a spring break trip, Kendric Burney and myself took a trip to California to visit Omar Brown, a former UNC football player. On the trip, Brown swiped his credit card for our hotel room. We later reimbursed him in cash. Burney gave me his part of the cash, and I gave Brown back the full reimbursement. The NCAA claimed I received "preferential treatment" because Brown originally paid for our hotel room. This fell under an "improper benefits" violation. As a consequence, I was suspended for the first four games of the 2010 season.

Brown and I had a big brother—little brother relationship during my time at UNC— him being a former UNC safety and me being a budding UNC safety. I sought his mentorship about handling the demands of being a star student-athlete. Thus, I did not believe this to be an issue. Since I had befriended Brown after enrolling at UNC as a student-athlete, the NCAA said that our relationship did not fulfill the "preexisting relationship clause" governed by the NCAA that would have totally absolved me from the alleged violation. In addition to the suspension, the NCAA forced me to pay a restitution of $450.67.

After being reinstated, I told the local newspaper:

> I always believe that everything that happens in your life is according to God's plan and that it's all going to work out for the good . . . I really think that going through that whole process, it made me appreciate playing and made me appreciate this time that I have here left [*sic*] much more.[18]

★ ★ ★

The accusations made by the NCAA left a dark cloud over the program and the players singled out in the investigation. I loved my teammates. We had a lot of players on the 2010 team who were the top football players in their respective positions in the country. If it were not for the NCAA violations that led to the suspensions of some of our best players, I honestly thought we could have been one of the best teams in college football and could have possibly won a national championship. This possibility was one of the main reasons for returning to play my senior year.

I was disappointed in the way UNC handled the investigation. I believe at the beginning of the investigation, they did not strongly support nor defend the players implicated. There should have been a unified front on the part of the university, the athletic department, and players when the NCAA wanted to investigate the football program. Instead, the university worked closely with the NCAA who, I believe, overstepped their boundaries.

There were other players around the country being investigated by the NCAA during the same time period, and it seemed as if their respective universities took a stance against the NCAA instead of inviting them in to cause havoc. Take, for example, AJ Green from the University of Georgia who was accused and later found guilty of selling his Independence Bowl jersey for $1000. He received support from his university before the NCAA suspended him for four games.

Instead of forming a unified front, it seemed as if UNC said one thing in front of the cameras, but behind closed doors it was a different story. While we now know that some players had violated NCAA rules, the university administration, athletic director, and coaching staff did not know that at the time. We were being investigated for "suspicion" of potential NCAA violations. The NCAA investigation was going to result in suspensions but not everyone was guilty of a violation. Although our former athletic director, Dick Baddour, called many of the suspensions "unduly harsh" and said appeals were forthcoming, the NCAA emphatically declared that their governing body had already ruled on all reinstatement requests made by UNC.[19] Thus, UNC had already, behind closed institutional doors, condemned those who they believed were guilty of NCAA violations.[20] My case was one of the appeals heard, although it fell on deaf ears.

In June of 2010, our football team had a meeting with the administration and coaches to explain in detail how both entities, the NCAA and UNC, would handle the investigation. I remember sitting in the meeting perplexed. I, as well as my teammates, had no clue what the investigation meant for our future playing status at UNC. Throughout my years at UNC, I can remember the team meeting as a group with the university administration, athletic director, and coaching staff to discuss concerns. However, this meeting was vastly different in tone and nature. The tension in the room was very thick. The administration was acting stiff and standoffish. Our coaches seemed very uncomfortable. This was one of the most unsettling meetings that I have ever been in.

After the administration left the meeting room and it was just the coaching staff and the football team, our coaches ended up separating us into assigned groups. They announced that everyone could leave the room with their assigned groups except for a few of us. I was one of the few. I stood there with the remaining teammates wondering what was going on and why we would be singled out—-all outwardly treated as guilty until proven innocent.

The investigation was one of the most degrading experiences during my time at UNC. The university had empowered the NCAA. The NCAA had us sign documentation that would essentially lead to us surrendering our rights to privacy. I had to turn over my bank account records, my cellphone records, and the username and password to all of my email accounts. At the end of the first meeting, I was asked to hand over my cellphone for them to go through my call list, text messages, and pictures. This was a full on assault of my privacy. This is what an NCAA investigation feels like for student-athletes.

Many of the players being investigated felt like the NCAA overstepped their bounds. We had all heard and read stories about how the NCAA is a corrupt revenue-generating machine that will find fault against anyone who they deem to be guilty of making monies outside of their conglomerate. In my opinion, their treatment was hypocritical because we know that the NCAA is a big corporation that manages a ton of smaller corporations (i.e., university and college teams and the student-athletes). The institutional structure of college sports generates billions of dollars from the usage of student-athletes, which not only profits the universities and colleges, but other public and private companies. Yet, the student-athlete is forbidden from profiting economically off of his or her athletic skills and talents, image, and likeness.

For instance, in the 2011—2012 academic year after the investigation became very public, the NCAA reported its revenue as $871.6 million.[21] *Business Insider* estimated in 2015 that the fair market value for the average NCAA Football Bowl Subdivision (Division I-A) player is worth $149,569 per year.[22] In return for our work and the revenue we generate for them, student-athletes are paid in the form of room, board, and tuition on year-to-year contracts called "scholarships." This system is exploitative and not equitable to the billions of dollars that student-athletes generate for the NCAA.

* * *

There was a weird feeling that overtook our football team. Those who were not under investigation responded in one of two ways: some empathized with us while others were upset that looming suspensions would ruin the upcoming football season. I was asked repeatedly about the NCAA investigation. But at the first meeting with the NCAA, they explicitly told us not to discuss the allegations with anyone. Do not tell anyone what is taking place—not my Nana, not my mother, not my uncles, and definitely not my coaches and teammates. We were being held to secrecy.

I was under the impression that their mission was to divide and conquer us. The NCAA tried to isolate each of us as much as possible until the final judgment was rendered to those under investigation. Meanwhile, every time I turned on ESPN there was some news story about the UNC football players who were under investigation. The media appeared to know more about what was actually happening than any of the players involved.

The NCAA investigation was an extremely tough situation to endure. One moment we were considered amateur football players at UNC, and then the next moment when we stepped out of the local grocery store, microphones and cameras were being shoved in our faces asking us to answer questions about the investigation. The worst part about all of this was knowing that my family and friends back in Jacksonville were hearing the same things from the news and having to deal with the local news asking them questions that they did not have the answers to.

After the four game suspension came down, my name was removed from the lists of awards that I could have been nominated for entering my senior year: The Ronnie Lott Award, The Jim Thorpe Award, and Pre-Season All-American honors. This was one of the lowest points in my career. My world was spinning out of control without football as my solace.

I'll Take AFAM for a "Paper Grade"

The NCAA investigation involving football players taking "improper benefits" only scratched the surface of the lack of institutional control that was supposedly rampant at UNC. The investigation into "improper benefits" escalated into an investigation about "academic misconduct." On August 26, 2010, the NCAA began a separate investigation into football players and other student-athletes taking "paper classes." The new set of allegations further tarnished the UNC football program.

To be clear, before we throw stones at UNC only, universities and colleges have always provided student-athletes the ability to take so-called "easy" college courses to remain academically eligible and/or to lighten an athlete's academic workload for decades as a normal practice. These institutions have facilitated a culture that allows some student-athletes to major in the discipline of "Eligibility" rather than adhering to a specific curriculum within a given academic discipline to ensure graduation. The goals of the institution and student-athlete are different sides of the same coin: First, the institution provides the opportunity to the student-athlete to take the easy college course for a high grade to remain academically eligible. Second, student-athletes take courses to remain academically eligible, and then focus the majority of their time on improving his or her athletic skills to benefit the team and the school. For the student-athletes trying to fulfill their collegiate obligation before going pro, this scenario works out beautifully; however, not every person who takes advantage of these easier courses has the same agenda.

The NCAA investigation into the accommodating college courses provided no substantial new revelation. The most shocking parts about it were the length of time the academic scheme had continued and the sole academic discipline involved. From 1993 to 2011, athletic programs at UNC used the African and Afro-American studies department

(AFAM) to provide "paper classes" to student-athletes to help guarantee their academic eligibility. The irony of all of this is that mostly black student-athletes were taking the courses. Of the 78 academic disciplines offered to undergraduates on campus, black student-athletes contributed significantly to watering down a major that just a few decades ago universities and colleges in the U.S. were opposed to even having on campus. The discipline of AFAM had much to offer us in terms of learning our history and culture and forbidding the cycle of becoming mis-educated at a PWI.

Most of the "paper classes" were advertised as traditional college courses but almost never met face-to-face and were graded essentially based on an end of the semester research paper. The "paper classes" awarded high passing grades to student-athletes with no regard for the quality of the presented work.[23] Available data obtained from the NCAA showed that from 2007 to 2011 alone, more than 67 percent of the AFAM courses were made up of student-athletes.[24] There were unauthorized grades, forged faculty signatures, and almost never any class time.

In the beginning of the investigation, the NCAA focused on the former Chair of the AFAM department, Professor Julius Nyang'oro, and his administrative assistant, Deborah Crowder. Initially, the NCAA believed they were the only two people involved in creating and encouraging "paper classes" for student-athletes. The NCAA later learned that an elaborate systematic scheme was in place, operating with the assistance of key personnel on campus.

Nyang'oro "taught" AFAM courses and gave students high passing grades for courses that rarely met or did not meet at all. Even more egregious was the fact that he empowered Crowder to over-enroll student-athletes in "paper classes" and even allowed her to grade papers. This was problematic for two reasons: First, she was not qualified to grade college-level work. Second, she was a big UNC basketball and football fan, which meant she had personal feelings at stake in the outcome of games.

Some folks have speculated that Nyang'oro did not know that Crowder was creating "paper classes," over-enrolling student-athletes, and giving inflated grades. In spite of this, when Nyang'oro did discover these things he did nothing to remedy the problems. To add insult to injury, when Crowder announced her retirement from UNC amidst the allegations, student-athletes got word of it and there was a spike in enrollment for AFAM courses during her last semester.

For a long time, UNC insisted that the problem was only with Nyang'oro and Crowder; however, this was far from the truth. In fact, the entire AFAM department was guilty of passing student-athletes so they could remain academically eligible.

The dots really connected when the NCAA found that "athletics personnel" were also involved in the scheme. They were alleged to have helped student-athletes register for easy courses to make passing grades. The NCAA generalized this issue to be attached to "athletics personnel," but in fact, it was the academic support personnel. These staff members worked for the Academic Support Program for Student-Athletes (ASPSA).

Many believed that the academic support personnel were doing their job. They were helping students sign up for courses and ensuring they were academically successful. The real problem was that the support personnel knew the courses offered by the AFAM department were easy and often had student-athletes sign up for them if their eligibility was in jeopardy or close to that point.

★ ★ ★

The NCAA made substantial claims against Nyang'oro, who is an African male, and Crowder, who is a white female, for their construction of the academic scheme and for providing easy "paper classes." To save their own hides, UNC officials and an UNC-sanctioned investigation initially said Crowder did nothing wrong and she was merely helping students. Former Governor James Martin, whose team of officials led the UNC investigation, said Crowder could be described as "Lady Liberty."[25] Records show that, "More than 3,100 students, 47.6 percent of them athletes, were enrolled in and received credit for the phantom classes, most of which were created and graded solely by [Crowder]".[26] She was indeed a part of the problem.

The governor even said to UNC trustees in front of UNC officials and reporters, "This was not an athletic scandal. It was an academic scandal, which is worse; but, an isolated one."[27] From the investigation into "improper benefits" to "paper classes," he wanted to do his part to preserve the reputation of the state's flagship university and himself while ousting the players involved in both scandals.

The ripple effect of these findings led Crowder to retire in 2009. Nyang'oro was forced to retire in 2012 and eventually charged with felony fraud. It was learned that in the summer of 2011, Nyang'oro received $12,000 to teach a course filled with football players that did not meet. A grand jury later indicted him. The felony charge carried up to ten months in prison if convicted. In 2014, charges were dropped after Nyang'oro cooperated with the investigation into "paper classes."

The problems related to the academic misconduct were shown to be much deeper when university learning specialist, Mary Willingham, found through her research that student-athletes on campus were performing far below their supposed academic level. In a CNN report, she explained that some UNC student-athletes could not read beyond an eighth-grade level. In some cases, they could not even read at a fifth-grade level, yet they were being passed along in most of their college courses.[28] She revealed that many athletic staff members knew about the "paper classes" and would openly discuss these courses as a strategy to maintain an athlete's eligibility.

In March of 2014, I took part in an ESPN's *Outsides the Lines* (OTL) interview that discussed the academic misconduct. Initially, I had mixed feelings about doing the interview. My intent was not to point the finger or indict; but rather, to help spotlight a glaring problem on university and college campuses where systematic structures are in place not to help all student-athletes graduate but to simply keep us eligible to play, thus enriching the institution. I did not participate in the interview because I sought to shatter personal relationships with family, friends, coaches, teammates, players from other sports at UNC, or even the mascot. Above all, I did not want to severe ties with UNC. In spite of my feelings about how the university handled the investigation of "improper benefits," it did open its doors to me for which I will always be grateful. Although I took part in the "paper classes" fiasco, I now wanted to be a part of the solution.

In the interview, I explained that academic advisors encouraged us to take the "paper classes." I wanted to make clear that, "Their job isn't necessarily to make Deunta Williams a better person, a smarter person. Their job necessarily is to make sure I'm eligible to play."[29] I went on to add:

> I think the coaches knew enough to understand what was going on . . . I think they knew about the system itself, and if a guy was in trouble the immediate response was, 'Why not put him in a paper class where he can receive help, get an A or a B out of this class for writing a good paper.'[30]

Mary Willingham, who was also apart of the OTL interview, revealed that, "Athletes couldn't write a paper, they couldn't write a paragraph, they couldn't write a sentence yet. Some of these students could read maybe at a second or third grade level, but really that's—for an adult—that is considered illiterate."[31] Her comments further embarrassed the university and the student-athletes who took the AFAM courses.

The usage of "paper classes" was further confirmed when former UNC basketball player, Rashad McCants, told OTL that he believed such courses were apart of collegiate culture in general. He made the Dean's list in Spring 2005 taking "paper classes" and received straight-A grades. McCants took a total of 18 AFAM courses (i.e., 54 credit hours). Of the 18 courses, ten of his course grades were A's.[32] In the OTL interview, McCants said:

> I thought it was a part of the college experience, just like watching it on a movie from He Got Game or Blue Chips . . . When you get to college, you don't go to class, you don't do nothing, you just show up and play. That's

exactly how it was, you know, and I think that was the tradition of college basketball, or college, period, any sport. You're not there to get an education, though they tell you that.

You're there to make revenue for the college. You're there to put fans in the seats. You're there to bring prestige to the university by winning games.[33]

Even more explosive about McCant's comments was the fact that he implicated legendary UNC basketball coach, Roy Williams, by asserting that Coach Williams knew about the "paper classes." In response to McCant's claims, Coach Williams rebutted:

With respect to the comments made today, I strongly disagree with what Rashad [McCants] has said. In no way did I know about or do anything close to what he says and I think the players whom I have coached over the years will agree with me. I have spent 63 years on this earth trying to do things the right way and the picture he portrays is not fair to the university or me.[34]

Two things make the back and forth between McCants and Coach Williams interesting. First, Deborah Crowder was a big fan of the UNC basketball team. She bled Carolina Blue basketball. Throughout the years, Crowder would gain special access to university basketball games after forging relationships with some players. She also befriended personnel in the athletic office who provided her with preferential treatment for games.[35] Second, basketball is the premier sport at UNC. The men's basketball team has won seven national championships (1924, 1957, 1982, 1993, 2005, 2009, and 2017) throughout its history. The validation of such damaging accusations would sully the name of Coach Williams and the historic program.

* * *

The criticism from my appearance on OTL was widespread. Afterwards, former teammates called and texted to discuss their disappointment with the OTL interview. One former teammate called to tell me that I was "bitter" and "wished [I] had made it to the league." Another teammate blatantly cursed me out over the phone. The text messages were even more vicious. But I listened and allowed them to vent their frustrations because at the end of the day, they are all *still* my brothers. We fight, then we make amends.

During the OTL interview, I told the truth about what we were exposed to as student-athletes while at UNC. It was not a popular message to hear. I think the Carolina family as a whole just wanted this issue to go away.

North Carolina alumni and fans were also upset about my interview on OTL. I received hateful comments and potential threats. Some took to social media via Twitter to voice their disappointment:

> @_Elle_Spencer_: Wonder how much they paid Deunta Williams' trash a** to be on OTL?[36]

> @MSU_Corey_UNC: deunta williams got a nice check to snitch I presume[37]

> @iAmDJSmooth_: Deunta Williams also the same dude that was involved with receiving improper benefits but he speaks out about classes #ironic[38]

> @kp_smitty: Marry [sic] Willingham . . . Deunta Williams. .Now Rashad McCants. Damn u bitter f**ks leave my school alone and get on about ya bussiness, for real[39]

> @The_SpacePope: Rashad McCants and Deunta Williams . . . Snitches because their pro careers failed. And

I really liked Deunta Williams. . . . [40]

To some degree, I can understand the disappointment from the Carolina faithful. During the nearly hour-long interview, OTL framed the segment, spliced certain portions of my interview, and shaped it for their own agenda. The interview did not completely convey the message I wanted to disseminate to the masses. I felt that my message got lost in their translation. All in all, the network did what I needed them to do, and that was to have an open discussion about the issue. Through other TV interviews, radio interviews, panel discussions, and behind the scenes conversations, I believe that I was able to communicate the student-athlete's side of the "paper classes" scandal.

To all of my fellow black student-athletes from UNC reading this book who continue to be angry, upset, disappointed, or believe that I have broken the infamous "no snitching code" by speaking out about this issue, we are mature adults now. In our pursuit to remain academically eligible by taking "paper classes," the university failed us, and we failed ourselves. We were misguided, young adults back then.

The truth about the state of academic affairs at UNC was completely unacceptable and embarrassing. We have to acknowledge this as people who once represented UNC in our respective sports. Not all black student-athletes knew about the "paper classes," but a large number of us did. Nonetheless, UNC should have dealt with Nyang'oro, Crowder, the AFAM department, and the athletic staff members who were complicit a long time ago.

★ ★ ★

Notwithstanding all of the bad blood that has come from the academic misconduct involving "paper classes," hopefully the outcomes will make UNC a better place for student-athletes, especially black student-athletes. This soapbox that I am standing on to deliver this message is not to make excuses about my part in all of this. I hold myself culpable in the "paper classes" scandal because I took full advantage of the system. To be honest, I knew when I was presented with the opportunity to take the "paper classes" that it was a dip below the academic standard I had set for myself prior to coming to UNC.

I knew when I signed my letter of intent that I had the opportunity to play major Division I-A football against some of the best competition in the country. I equally understood that I had an opportunity to earn a world-class education during my tenure at UNC. When the "paper classes" were presented as an option, I instantly knew that enrolling in them would be taking a shortcut.

To the defense of student-athletes who were faced with the same decision, there are many unbeknownst pressures associated with the decision to take "paper classes." Being a student-athlete is like being a superhero; by day you push your brain to its learning limits and by night you push your body to its physical limits. Furthermore, if you decide that going to the NFL is your goal, then you must put in even more time towards your sport.

In a 2014 radio interview with Adam Gold and Joe Ovies on 99.9 FM, I described the demands of playing college football and the amount of "athlete time" needed to keep up on the academic side. Consequently, these types of courses are in place for student-athletes but rarely lead them to matriculate from college:

> There is a system of things going on where players don't necessarily have enough time [to take rigorous courses]. So systems, like whatever was going on at Carolina, are created. Not just at Carolina but across the country, where people are taking basket weaving, or you're taking a hard class load during the offseason and during the season you're taking an easy one.[41]

Those looking from the outside have to remember that there are no "full" scholarships, only year-to-year contracts for those with unfilled potential to tap into that potential to maximize the student-athletes' skills and talents. This symbiotic relationship benefits both parties: you help the university win games and earn revenue, and capitalize on the chance for a future professional payday. On the football team, we talked often in the locker room about "making it" and "taking care of our families" and "never having to worry about being broke again." These were real conversations that became real goals.

★ ★ ★

Many of the black student-athletes at UNC who participated in the "paper classes" lost the opportunity to take full advantage of getting a college degree regardless of the indentured servitude of the contract scholarships. Black student-athletes from 1993 to 2011 who no longer play professional sports for a salary and those who only played college sports and returned to their hometowns afterwards, often left the university with no college degree. One of my teammates, Michael McAdoo, who played football from 2008 to 2010 filed a class-action lawsuit against UNC admitting he and other black student-athletes who were encouraged to take "paper classes" were cheated out of getting a "legitimate education."

I wish there was more institutional control in place. I wish the academic shortcut did not exist. I wish we had not taken the academic shortcut. I wish the "Big Business of College Athletics" allowed student-athletes the time to be the very best students that they can be as well as the very best athletes they can be. Too many student-athletes, in general, are tempted to take academic short cuts.

We know that there is a significant drop off in the percentage of black student-athletes who graduate from college in comparison to our white counterparts. It is important that we use the system and not allow the system to use us. We must use our athletic skills and talents to earn an education and provide a better quality of life for our families. This is how you win in the game of life as a student-athlete. As Lettermen and Letterwomen of UNC, our promise now should be to mentor and provide support for the next generation of black student-athletes.

Lots of former black student-athletes still show up to the Carolina vs. Duke men's basketball game at the Dean E. Smith Center and the Carolina vs. North Carolina State football game at Kenan Memorial Stadium——both are big sporting events often televised in front of a national audience on one of the major networks. Yet, the biggest show at Kenan Memorial Stadium happens during commencement season every December and May. It is a packed house to see you walk across the stage and receive your college diploma. For many of us, it will be (and was) the last cheers we hear from the stands.

CHAPTER 4
PRACTICING THE POWER OF COURAGE:
ADVICE FROM THE SIDELINE

Deuteronomy 31:6 reads, "Be strong and courageous. Do not be afraid or terri-
fied because of them, for the Lord your God goes with you; He will never leave
you nor forsake you."

Psalm 23: 4 reads, "Even though I walk through the darkest valley, I will fear
no evil, for you are with me; your rod and your staff, they comfort me."

I find courage in the above messages. Courage resides within each and
every person. It is the ability to persevere and be resilient in the face
of adversity. There are different types of courage: emotional, moral,
physical, and spiritual courage. Growing up in the Sandy Run Projects
in Jacksonville, NC, I observed courage to be the resolve of my mother
to make a way for us. When I finally met my father, I observed courage
in facing the man who I did not believe existed until the age of 15. As a
former college athlete who played sports his entire life until the injury, I
observed courage to be associated with physical attributes and bravery.
When I was declared medically unable to return to football and not
drafted by the NFL, while harboring feelings of fear and uncertainty, I
observed courage to be simply waking up each day and trying to recov-
er from my broken life. After I made the decision to speak out against
"paper classes" to spotlight a glaring problem on university and college
campuses, I observed courage as the ability to stand up for injustice and
speak an unfavorable truth.

The advice presented in this chapter is to help a person along their journey in life. These pieces of advice represent what I believe to be the best strategies——for athletes and non-athletes alike—— to practice as they master the power of courage. A critical aspect of the power of courage is acknowledging fear. One would have no need for courage if fear were never present. Fear, however, is not something that should be looked at as a negative aspect of the power of courage. In fact, it would be wise to view fear as the catalyst that sparks the chain reaction leading to courage—— the "call to action." In this moment, fear can either hold you back or can cause you to call upon your inner courage to take action. In order to progress in life and in order to overcome the breaking points we face in life, you must call upon your courage.

1. Have the Courage to Be True to Thy Self:

Getting through my breaking point was an emotional experience in so many ways. I really felt like I let my family down——my nuclear, extended, and Jacksonville, NC family. I love my city and I feel the love back from the people. Many were rooting and pulling for me; however, I let myself down.

I became so invested in Deunta Williams, the football player, that Deunta Williams, the person, was secondary to my life. In simpler terms, I had only invested in my ego. The biggest struggle I had was facing my ego. I loved this person created by my ego. My ego had a lot of friends, was very popular, and was very valuable. My ego was wrapped up in the persona of being a star athlete likely headed to "The League." When I broke my leg, my ego broke with it. I felt as though I no longer had an identity. These feelings intensified when a lot of my so-called friends disappeared. A lot of the ladies I thought loved me for me moved on to the next budding star. I went from "the man" to a "has-been" in a very short amount of time in the eyes of many people. My bright star had dimmed. I was hopelessly looking for my "true" identity. Questions like, "Where did it go?" and "Who am I now?" haunted me for the longest time.

Admittedly, I had a difficult time practicing courage at first. I tried to deal with my identity crisis the cowardly way. To compensate, I would invest in superficial items and participate in superficial activities. For instance, I remember purchasing a Porsche Panamera and BMW X6 with 24inch rims on it. For some reason, buying these superficial items gave me great comfort because they cemented my place in the big American Dream. After the injury I still wanted to be thought of in the same manner, and for a brief moment, the attention and looks I received reminded me of my days as a ball player. This simple, yet fleeting pleasure, was enough to satisfy my insatiable ego from time to time. In my alone time, I was still haunted by the brokenness inside of me.

There was an unsettled lack of peace within myself. In most cases, people dealing with extreme internal conflict choose to hide it from their loved ones and I was no different. I hid this lifestyle filled with coping mechanisms from my family and closest friends. On paper, I was young, decent-looking, making good money, and considered successful but internally I was still broken.

My "aha moment" came when my then-business mentor, Tom Little, a successful, older, white man, who owned many different businesses, complimented me on my Porsche Panamera. During the conversation, he asked why I would purchase such an expensive vehicle. I was initially confused as to why anyone of his stature would not want a luxury car such as a Porsche Panamera. Tom went on to explain that he too grew up not having much, but did not have to possess superficial items to validate his worth or stroke his ego.

We eventually moved on from that part of the conversation but I was convicted by his comments. It started a life overhaul. I had to ask myself, "who was I trying to impress by buying these luxury items and why?" I spent so many years trying to satisfy my ego that Deunta, the country boy from Jacksonville, had gotten lost in the maze of acceptance. This life assessment was a major breakthrough for me because it helped me to look in the mirror. I sat back and analyzed the course of decisions that led me to this point.

At this point, I had plenty of luxury items in my life: nice cars, clothes, jewelry, and a high-rise condo in Buckhead Atlanta, GA. I began to notice that I had an infatuation with these luxury items. I viewed this period in my life as being stuck in the rat race; and thus, constantly chasing pieces of cheese only to collect them and still feel empty on the inside.

There was fear associated with the new realization of my thoughts. Since I was living "the life," I feared what others would think about me downsizing my lifestyle. They would say, "Oh, he's broke now." Or, "He's just like the other athletes who spent all of their money." Needless to say, I worried that downsizing would sully my reputation. That is, my ego.

One of the tougher parts of being true to myself was being delivered from other people's opinions and judgments. So many of us care about the gossip and rumors spread about us or are concerned about what people are saying privately. We sometimes fall victim to portraying or projecting to be a certain type of person in order to control the narrative surrounding our lives. The truth of the matter is, people are going to talk about you, me, or anyone else without us being able to control the narrative. Therefore, with this bold understanding, we must be true to thy self.

I did not truly know my self-worth to the world without football. In the chase to make it to "The League," there was never a discovery of my self-worth. Football provided self-triumph but not self-worth. Self-Triumph is reached from a victory or major achievement. The victories and major achievements felt good but there was never the feeling of understanding my true self-worth. I have come to realize that when you are chasing something you are not totally aware of your presence within the moment. The moment can overshadow your self-worth and eventually lead to self-defeat. The injury forced me to be in the present and face this new adversity. As American televangelist, Robert H. Schuller, is known for saying, "Tough times never last, but tough people do."

2. Have the Courage to Listen When Life Talks:

One of the original chapters I wrote for this book was titled, "Follow the Tumbleweeds." Within this chapter, I set out to mimic the opening scenes of an old western movie. In western movies, the opening scene is usually shot in a desert-like setting while the wind blows with a few tumbleweeds gusting across the desert. In the direction of the blowing tumbleweed, you find the saloon, and then the movie begins. For me, this has always been very strong imagery. The tumbleweeds are evidence that the winds of change are blowing, and if you are intuitively connected, you will pay attention.

Metaphorically and personally, this scene can be connected to the 2010 Franklin American Mortgage Music City Bowl. Days before the Music City Bowl against the Tennessee Volunteers, I recall meeting an elderly man by happenstance and having a heart-to-heart conversation with him about life's trials and tribulations.

In our conversation, he openly told me that he was terminally ill. He had a brain tumor. Doctors told the elderly man that he had about three months or so to live. He was just living out the rest of his days on earth. And one of his last moments on earth, he shared with me.

To my amazement, the anticipation of death gave him a sense of calmness. It was extremely humbling to be in his presence and talk to him about life. He talked, and I listened. He spoke about the "winds of change" and how he dealt with them in his latter years while dealing with his illness. He told me about his life and all the things he had accomplished. I talked, and then he listened. I told him about all of my big dreams. There was a kindred connection brewing during the conversation.

The kindred connection that emerged from our conversation remained with me after we left each other's presence. The words of our conservation were later revealed when I was in the locker room during halftime of the Music City Bowl. Sitting there in tears with my lower right leg broken, I thought about our conversation. The irony is that a complete stranger had given me the positive mental frame and energy needed in a critical moment of my life. As I heard the oohh's and aahh's of the crowd and Drew Davis, the coach's son, going back and forth from the locker room and reporting to me the score of the game in the 3rd and 4th quarters, I used the substance from the conversation with the elderly man to gain a sense of calm. Within that trying moment, I realized that I was down, but not out.

The conservation with the elderly man was God's way of "winking" at me. We can often find God in all things. Looking at this complete stranger facing his death with courage, strength, and dignity, gave me courage. To this day, I continue to believe that our conversation was God's own way of saying to me, "Life is short. Expect the unexpected. Nothing is guaranteed. Do not allow adversity to break you. Find a way to breakthrough."

When life speaks to you, you must listen. Do not live your life oblivious to its ever-changing winds. Notice the signs that life is giving and learn how to adapt rather than holding onto the things of your past. This piece of advice is universal. It can be applicable to an athlete, as well as, a businessperson. In my business life, I have learned that industry standards and best practices shift constantly. It is those who are able to foresee these changes that are able to quickly adapt to remain successful. Just like in sports, you have to be a student of the game of life in order to win abundantly.

3. Have the Courage to Practice the 3 C's:
Commitment, Consistency, and Change of Mentality

Have you ever felt as if you wanted more out of life? In the past, I have felt this way many times. Growing up, when my mother could not afford to buy my brother and I the nicest pair of tennis shoes, I felt this way. When I would visit my childhood friend's house and compared their living condition to my own, I felt this way. Even when I went to UNC and saw my peers driving fancy cars bought by their parents versus the 12-year-old hooptie I drove that had to be fixed every two to three weeks, I felt this way.

The question that formulates when I think back on those times in my life is, "how does a person conquer the feeling of wanting more out of life?" Action must be taken. In order to conquer this feeling, a person must rely on the three C's: *Commitment, Consistency, and Change of Mentality:*

- First, a person must *commit* himself or herself to a specific goal. *Commitment* will motivate a person to get out of the bed in the morning with their mind set on working on their goal. A commitment to changing your situation simply starts with a conversation with yourself. During the conversation, you must determine that you are not satisfied with where you are at in your life and ready for a change. This conversation with yourself often leads you to make a life decision. This life decision leads to a "commit to the action" to change your current situation.
- Second, a person must be *consistent* in their pursuit of the goal. The only difference between people who reach their goals and those who do not reach their goals is that one set of people did not quit when they encounter failure and the other set did. *Consistency* will ensure that the person is closer to accomplishing the goal.
- Last, *consistency* breeds a mentality to *change* the way in which that person interprets the workload associated with accomplishing their goal. They begin to develop a workmanlike/ workwomanlike mentality. When there is a *change of mentality*, a person will now confidently believe that it is possible to achieve any goal.

For me, after the crazy partying sessions, which consisted of girls, alcohol, and drugs, I *committed* myself to a specific goal. That goal was to become an entrepreneur. The first step was to enroll in an MBA program. Enrolling into the program turned out to be my best post-college decision. During my tenure as a graduate student, I became a knowledgeable and resourceful entrepreneur who would later become a successful entrepreneur.

The second step was to be *consistent*. In the pursuit of my MBA, there was a ton of *consistency* needed to complete my workload. It was a fulltime workload for almost two years. This continued even after I graduated. I had to figure out that learning business and doing business are two entirely different things. I had to practice *consistency* in learning how to operate a business.

In order to become a successful entrepreneur, it takes relentless effort and hard work, but also important, is finding a way to reinterpret the workload associated with building a successful business (i.e., 24/7 hours—no vacations—no sick days). When there was a *change of mentality*, I was able to handle the rigors of the business world more effectively and efficiently. Before my change, I had urges to go and party or waste time. When my *mentality changed*, I was able to build multiple successful business endeavors.

4. Have the Courage to Have a Multitude of Council:
The Four Corners

"There is safety in a multitude of council." In this manner, I consult with a number of people in my life to deliberate and come to a conclusion on a decision of great consequence. I have come to find that successful people lean on and trust each other and at a given time provide each other with invaluable advice.

The fear, however, you must overcome in order to have a multitude of council is the fear of vulnerability. Receiving council from a multitude of people can be very difficult because none of us enjoy the feeling of being judged. To overcome this feeling, it is important to figure out who you can and who you cannot be open and vulnerable with. In order to competently execute the power of a multitude of council, you will have to surround yourself with more than one person to make the most informed and balanced decisions.

I have developed a strategy for making big decisions in my life. I call it the *Four Corners* strategy. The strategy is simple. I have four people who I seek advice from before I make any major decision. Their advice helps me sort through the information, see it with clarity, and ultimately make the most informed and balanced decision regarding an issue, concern, or business endeavor. I trust each of them. As a result, I am able to be completely honest and transparent with them, giving them all the pertinent details about the sorting of the information to make the decision.

These four personal advisors come from different walks of my life. Some represent where I have come from in my life, and others represent where I would like to go in my life. These two points of enlightenment—where I have come from and where I would like to go— are usually major factors influencing my decisions. These councilors serve as my motivators, my advisors, and most important, my voices of reason.

In my opinion, when you have four people from different walks of life who can give you advice from different perspectives, it leads to making the most informed and balanced decisions. I know that at the end of the day, I am solely responsible for the decision to be made. Nevertheless, their input has helped to make all the difference in a lot of endeavors in my life. This practice helps to improve my decision-making process and the quality of my decision.

5. Have the Courage to Become Successful:

SUCCESS: The accomplishment of an aim or purpose; a person or thing that achieves a desired aim and attains prosperity.[42]

This piece of advice comes from my personal experiences with extremely successful people. In the 21st century, the new reality of success is faking it until you actually make it. People have the tendency to chase success via superficial items to outwardly prove to others that they are successful. The ideology of success is aligned with people buying and showing superficial items as signs of accomplishment and riches. These people are chasing success through appearance rather than working diligently to become successful through hard work.

This false perception of success can lie to us because we know that you cannot always judge a book by its cover. This false perception of success can distract us from our main goal, which is to actually become successful. The chase of success is often why it eludes some of us. Some project the illusion of success rather than taking the time to ensure that they become successful.

There is a reason that successful people such as Arthur Ashe have said that, "Success is a journey not a destination. The doing is usually more important than the outcome. Not everyone can be Number 1." You can chase success all day long, either you will attain it or you will not attain it, but becoming successful comes from the "doing." Those who chase success view the journey as a long-drawn-out process. Those who do the "doing" know that the journey is necessary to become successful.

The people who decide to stop chasing success and learn how to become successful have all experienced elevated levels of success in all of their ventures. More than likely, this dramatic change began with the *changing of their mentality*, which leads to a paradigm shift.

For me, the transition from chasing success to becoming successful started with first getting to know myself, and then being true to myself. This process really woke me up and helped me to gain a new purpose. I then followed the three C's: *Commitment, Consistency, and Change of Mentality* and during this process was shown my capabilities as a human being. Instead of waking up and wasting time in the morning, I knew I needed to get up and go workout. After my workout, shower, and breakfast, I had to start my workday, which at the time was a mixture of graduate school, coaching, and visiting rehabilitation houses to mentor others. My life steadily became a routine of positive habits to improve my life and the lives of those around me. This manifested in bigger and better things.

In short, I learned how to become successful by "doing." I was no longer chasing it. Success takes time. Success takes patience. Success demands that a person stay the course and believe in the process. This is how you *become successful*. I promise that the process is well-worth the sacrifice and hard work. Successful people breathe, talk, and walk in a successful manner. They have an air of confidence about themselves because they know what you do not know. They know that they have been working tirelessly on the goal of becoming successful, and above all, they are prepared to reap the benefits and rewards of their efforts.

COURAGE EXERCISE

Courage resides within each and every person. Research studies have shown that the most effective way to overcome your fears in life are to face them head-on. Write down five of your fears in detail and identify a positive strategy to combat said fear. In the inspirational words of Anaïs Nin, "Life shrinks or expands in proportion to one's courage."

1. Fear

_____

Positive Strategy

_____

_____

_____

_____

_____

_____

_____

_____

_____

_____

_____

_____

_____

_____

2. Fear

_____

Positive Strategy

_____

_____

_____

_____

_____

_____

_____

_____

_____

_____

_____

_____

_____

_____

3. Fear

_____

Positive Strategy

_____

_____

_____

_____

_____

_____

_____

_____

_____

_____

_____

_____

_____

_____

4. Fear

_____

Positive Strategy

_____

_____

_____

_____

_____

_____

_____

_____

_____

_____

_____

_____

5. Fear

_____

Positive Strategy

_____

_____

_____

_____

AFTERWORD
BIG TICKET OUT OF THE HOOD

Thank you all for reading *My Breaking Point*. From the start to the final manuscript, writing this book has been an amazing creative process. If you have just finished reading this, then I have a very strong message for you: **Believe in the impossible!** This is the big takeaway away from the book.

When I was a kid, I imagined doctors, lawyers, teachers, coaches, and even people on TV to be extraordinary people. I never imagined that a kid born into poverty from the Sandy Run Projects could be extraordinary as well. That idea seemed to be an impossible feat to transition in life from irrelevant (i.e., poor kid from the projects) to relevant (i.e., author, motivational speaker, entrepreneur, public figure).

I considered this feat to be impossible for two reasons: First, I considered myself to be an ordinary, humble, and God-fearing guy. I did not believe that these were the characteristics of being extraordinary. The mirror of life reflected a different type of person in the hood. Black masculinity reigned supreme. I thought I had to act a certain way, talk a certain way, and walk a certain way for people to respect me. Little did I know at the time, being an ordinary, humble, and God-fearing guy was the exact mixture of characteristics that would lead me to extraordinary.

Second, I was a black male born in the hood. I look at being born black in the hood as one of the lowest starting places in life. According to the 2010 U.S. Census, blacks were 13.6 percent of the U.S. population. Five percent of U.S. citizens were black males. We represent a small percentage in American society; however, we continue to be policed at an alarming rate, disproportionately incarcerated, disenfranchised by partial voting rights, and face institutional and systemic barriers that at times denies equal access to employment, job promotion, and formal education.

Despite all the trials and tribulations I have faced in my life, I stand as a black male who has achieved. I grew up in the hood surrounded by poverty, drugs, gangs, and violence but those negative forces were never pervasive enough to deter me from becoming successful. I used the sport of football as my "big ticket out of the hood."

I am glad to share my life with you through this book. I do not know what motivated you to pick up this book and read it. Maybe you are a family member, friend, fellow author, fellow motivational speaker, fellow entrepreneur, know me from my days of playing football at UNC, know me as a product of Jacksonville, NC, or maybe God placed this book in your hand. No matter the reason, I want to say "Thank you!" Thank you! Thank you! Thank you! I especially want to thank you because I know we have one thing in common: We both believe in the impossible!

Signed,
Just a kid from the Sandy Run Projects
Deunta Williams

ACKNOWLEDGEMENTS

The seeds planted to create and grow this work were deeply inspired by my life's trials and tribulations; every situation I have seen or have lived through in the course of my life thus far. For the good, I am grateful. For the bad, I am grateful. Through it all, I have learned how to always smile through the tears of joy and pain.

I believe in a higher power, and for me, I call him the Heavenly Father. God has been extremely faithful to my entire family and me. My faith in God has strengthened me in my darkest times and given me the ability to find peace in the midst of chaos.

There are two special ladies in my life: My Nana, my peace. My mother, my vibrant ball of light. I love you both with as much love as a son can have and give to his beautiful mothers. I am honored to be a part of your legacy.

As a kid, when I stayed with my Nana every day she would send me to the mailbox. When I returned, she would ask, "Was my million dollar check in the mailbox?" She still asks the same question to this day. Only by the grace of God, am I able to tell her today, "Nana, we have more than that now."

To my Uncle, my prophet, my OG, my first father, and my close councilor, I kept my solemn promise. Your leadership, guidance, and honesty have challenged me to embrace a unique life. I have said it before and I will say it again, when I get on my knees to pray, I thank God for Uncle B a.k.a Uncle Henry. I love you.

To my father, I remember the first time I wished you were my Dad. Dreams do come true. You have taught me that nothing in this world is perfect and that lesson has been a beautiful blessing. I have observed your strength and meekness and it has taught me how to carry myself as a man in this world. I take great pride in knowing that I am your son. I love you and always hold you in high regard.

To the late Eugene Parker a.k.a Frank Lucas, I miss you, man. I wish you could see how this book came together. R.I.P.

To my other family members, coaches, teammates, teachers, and friends, thank you for believing in me and encouraging me to go through with writing this book. You were right!

To my Carolina Family: Brotherhood, I greatly appreciate the love and support you gave to me. From taking a chance on a poor kid from Jacksonville, NC to being there for me when I broke my leg and beyond, I thank you for the continuous support. I learned about brotherhood, I learned about accountability, and more importantly, I learned about family. To the UNC fans, thank you for all of the well wishes. "A Tar Heel born, a Tar Heel bred, and when I die, a Tar Heel dead!"

ABOUT THE AUTHOR

Deunta Williams is an author, motivational speaker, entrepreneur, former college football All-American athlete, and youth advocate who epitomizes resilience. Growing up in a public housing project in Jacksonville, North Carolina, at an early age Deunta was exposed to immense poverty and a lack of educational resources. Despite his environment, Deunta had an insatiable desire for knowledge and a relentless commitment to overcoming obstacles in his path. After a notable high school career as a three-sport athlete playing football, basketball, and track, he selected a football scholarship to the University of North Carolina-Chapel Hill (UNC) from numerous scholarship offers. At UNC, Deunta's achievements continued when he reached All-American status and was projected as a top safety for the 2011 NFL Draft. These accolades, however, came to a screeching halt when Deunta broke his right lower leg in the last game of his collegiate career and was declared medically unable to return to football. This moment in time led to a breaking point. Instead of being broken, he viewed this breaking point as something positive and decided to practice acceptance of a new direction for his life. It is down this path of promise where he realized his life was bigger than football.

For more information about the author, please visit:
DeuntaWilliams.com

E.M.E.R.G.E.

Empowering Messages, Expanding Resources, Genuine Engagement

E.M.E.R.G.E. works with low income and minority youth who face challenges caused by social and economic deprivation. We offer multi-faceted programs that bring awareness to and combat the causes and consequences of achievement gaps. Achievement gap refers to the observed disparity of educational measures between groups of students; in comparison low income and minority youth score lower within these educational measures to their counterparts.

MISSION: To increase youth achievement and eliminate the growing achievement gap.

VISION: Underserved youth will have access to the American dream, be prepared to compete globally, and make positive contributions to the community and nation.

AIM: Provide and partner with proactive programs that focus on helping socially and economically deprived youth experience success in school and life.

GOAL: Establish equity-fairness in education, equal access to learning opportunities and greater equality in educational achievement, attainment and benefits.

For more information about E.M.E.R.G.E., please visit:
www.emerge4youth.org.

NOTES
(Endnotes)

1   See the 2011 NFL combine rating. Available at: http://www.nfl.com/combine/profiles/deunta-williams?id=2495246.

2   Unknown. 2010. "Deunta Williams exits with broken leg." *ESPN. com*. Available at: http://www.espn.com/college-football/bowls10/news/story?id=5971981 (December 31).

3   See Friedlander, B. 2011. "Deunta Williams has surgery on broken leg." *StarNewsOnline.com*. Available at: http://acc.blogs.starnewsonline.com/19439/deunta-williams-has-surgery-on-broken-leg (January 6).

4   *Ibid*, 2011 NFL combine rating

5   See InsideCarolinaDotCom (2011, February 27). InsideCarolina.com—NFL combine interview: Deunta Williams [Video file]. Retrieved from: https://www.youtube.com/watch?v=ihd1eZUd_aM.

6   *Ibid*, InsideCarolina.com—NFL combine interview: Deunta Williams

7   See Arthur, R. 2016. "The shrinking shelf life of NFL players." *WSJ.com*. Available at: https://www.wsj.com/articles/the-shrinking-shelf-life-of-nfl-players-1456694959 (February 29).

8   See the Oxford Dictionary of English. 3rd Revised Edition.

9   See Strauss, M. 2011. "UNC, S: Deunta Williams interview." *ProInterviews.com*. Available at: https://prointerviews.org/2011/04/26/deuntawilliams (April 26).

10   *Ibid*, UNC, S: Deunta Williams interview

11   See the blog post, "Anyone know what happened to Deunta Williams?" *BodyBuilding.com*. Available at: https://forum.bodybuilding.com/archive/index.php/t-136994793.html?s=d41891712af959ceb52b46f6b15ba0ef.

12   See the blog post, "Deunta Williams' football career is over (story

post #3)." *CowboysZone.com*. Available at: http://cowboyszone.com/threads/deunta-williams-football-career-is-over-story-post-3.228722.

13 *Ibid*, UNC, S: Deunta Williams interview

14 The Management and Society major is housed in the Department of Sociology.

15 See the UNC website. Available at: http://www.unc.edu/prospective-students.

16 A 3:07 a.m. time stamp was reported by many media outlets, however, Google's cached page indicates 6:07 a.m.

17 See Hille, B. 2017. "Former agent pleads guilty to giving cash to North Carolina football players." *SportingNews.com*. Available at: http://www.sportingnews.com/ncaa-football/news/former-agent-pleads-guilty-to-giving-cash-to-north-carolina-football-players/1l2wji1c2lbus1gs3fle7sakff (April 18).

18 Unknown. 2010. "Williams glad to be back with Tar Heels after suspension." *RockyMountTelegram.com*. Available at: http://www.rockymounttelegram.com/College/2010/10/14/Williams-glad-to-be-back-with-Tar-Heels-after-suspension.html (October 14).

19 Unknown. 2010. "Tar Heels' Burney, Williams penalized." *ESPN.com*. Available at: http://www.espn.com/college-football/news/story?id=5604590 (September 22).

20 The requests for reinstatement are available at: http://www.unc.edu/news/ncaa/nov2012/Requests%20for%20Reinstatement%20_%20released%2011%205%202012%20_%2076%20pages.pdf.

21 See the NCAA's website. Information available at: http://www.ncaa.org/about/resources/finances/revenue.

22 See Gaines, C. 2015. "The average University of Texas football player is worth $622,000 per year." *BusinessInsider.com*. Available at: http://www.businessinsider.com/college-football-player-value-2015–9 (September 22).

23 See Barnes, G. 2017. "Key figure in NCAA's UNC investigation Deborah Crowder responds." *Scout.com*. Available at: http://www.scout.com/college/north-carolina/story/1761435-crowder-responds (March 9).

24 See Baxter, B. 2012. "UNC football scandal reveals long history of academic fraud." *TheCollegeFix.com*. Available at: http://www.thecollegefix.com/post/11485 (August 24).

25 See Kane, D. 2014. "Deborah Crowder's story could bring NCAA investigators to UNC." *CharlotteObserver.com*. Available at: http://www.charlotteobserver.com/news/local/education/article9113093.html (April 15).

26 See Lyall, S. 2014. "U.N.C. investigation reveals athletes took fake classes." *NYTimes.com*. Available at: https://www.nytimes.com/2014/10/23/sports/university-of-north-carolina-investigation-reveals-shadow-curriculum-to-help-athletes.html (October 22).

27 See Kane, D. 2015. "Former Gov. Martin says he misspoke about UNC scandal." *NewsObserver.com*. Available at: http://www.newsobserver.com/news/local/education/unc-scandal/article28708351.html (July 25).

28 See Ganim, S. 2014. "CNN analysis: Some college athletes play like adults, read like 5th-graders." *CNN.com*. Available at: http://www.cnn.com/2014/01/07/us/ncaa-athletes-reading-scores/index.html (January 8).

29 See ESPN (2014, March 25). UNC academic scandal: Whistleblower, former athlete speak out [Video file]. Retrieved from: http://www.espn.com/video/clip?id=10671809.

30 *Ibid*, UNC academic scandal: Whistleblower, former athlete speak out

31 *Ibid*, UNC academic scandal: Whistleblower, former athlete speak out

32 See Delsohn, S. 2014. "UNC's McCants: 'Just show up, play.'" *ESPN.com*. Available at: http://www.espn.com/espn/otl/story/_/id/11036924/former-north-carolina-basketball-star-rashad-mccants-says-took-sham-classes (June 5).

33 *Ibid*, UNC's McCants: 'Just show up, play

34 *Ibid*, UNC's McCants: 'Just show up, play

35 *Ibid*, Deborah Crowder's story could bring NCAA investigators to UNC

36 See @ _Elle_Spencer_ (2014, March 25). Retrieved from: https://twitter.com/_elle_spencer_/status/448591846235574272.

37 See @ MSU_Corey_UNC (2014, March 28). Retrieved from: https://twitter.com/msu_corey_unc/status/449546948547444736.

38 See @ iAmDJSmooth_ (2014, March 28). Retrieved from:

https://twitter.com/iamdjsmooth_/status/449575060786143232.

39 See @ kp_smitty (2014, June 6). Retrieved from: https://twitter.com/kp_smitty/status/474957088603385858.

40 See @ The_SpacePope (2014, June 6). Retrieved from: https://twitter.com/the_spacepope/status/474948417735905280.

41 Unknown. 2014. "Former UNC player: Systematic problem between academics and athletics." *WralSportsFan.com*. Available at: http://www.wralsportsfan.com/former-unc-player-systematic-problem-between-academics-and-athletics/13527711 (March 31).

42 See the Oxford Dictionary of English. 3rd Revised Edition.

INDEX

A.
academic misconduct, 31, 36, 41, 44, 48
    and academic advisors, 43, 45
academic success, 30
accountability, 32, 70
adversity, 8,12
    from mother's letter, v
    and personal hurdles, 13-14, 52, 55, 57
African and Afro-American studies department (AFAM), 41-42, 43, 45, 48
American Dream, 2, 13, 54, 72
Ashe, Arthur, 61
Austin, Marvin, 35-36

B.
Bachelors degree, 11, 50
Baddour, Dick, 38
biological father, 17, 19-24
blog post, 10
Brown, Omar, 36-37
Burney, Kendric, 3, 36

C.
CNN report, 44
college education, 32, 49-50
    and advanced degrees, 11
Collins, Danine Dale, 15-16, 19
    relationship with son, 2, 6, 13, 18-30, 35, 40, 52, 57, 69

being a single mother, 19

courage, 52-53

and being true to thy self, 53

and to listen when life talks, 55, 57

and to practice the 3 C's, 57

and to have a multitude of council, 59

and to become successful, 60

Crowder, Deborah, 42-44, 46, 48

D.

Davis, Butch, 3

Davis, Drew, 3, 56

Dean E. Smith Center, 51

DeVry University, 11

Division I-A football, 27, 34-35, 49

E.

E.M.E.R.G.E. (Empowering Messages, Expanding Resources, Genuine Engagement), 11, 72

F.

Facebook, 35

faith in God, 5

fear, 52-53, 55, 59, 62

G.

grades, 27, 30, 42-45

graduation, 41

H.

high school football, 25-27

I.

improper benefits, 31, 36, 41, 44, 47

J.
Jacksonville, NC, 2-3, 6-8, 11, 13, 15, 17, 26, 30-31, 35, 40, 52-54, 68, 70
Jacksonville Daily News, 35

K.
Kenan Memorial Stadium, 36, 51

L.
Little, Greg, 36
Little, Tom, 54
Louisiana State University (LSU), 36

M.
Masters degree, 11
Martin, James, 43
medically unable, 8, 10-11, 16, 52, 71
 recheck, 5
McAdoo, Michael, 50
McCants, Rashad, 45-46
Mortgage Music City Bowl, 1, 56
motivation, 16, 25

N.
National Collegiate Athletic Association (NCAA), 1, 4, 8-10, 31-33, 35-43
National Football League (NFL), 1, 30, 49, 52-53, 55
 and combine and rating, iii, 4-5, 7
 and draft, 1-2, 4-7, 9-10, 16, 31
Nyang'oro, Julius, 42-44, 48

O.
Outsides the Lines (OTL), 44

P.
Parker, Eugene, 4-5

paper classes, 41-46, 48-50, 52
paternity test, 21-22
perseverance, v
poverty, 13, 17-19, 28
 poor-tential, 25, 27
predominantly white institution (PWI), 31, 42
preexisting relationship clause, 37
preferential treatment, 4, 31, 36, 46

Q.
Quinn, Robert, 7, 36

R.
redshirt, 33-35
Rivals All-American, 27
Roosevelt, Eleanor, 12

S.
Sandy Run Projects, 13, 15-17, 25, 31, 52, 67-68
Schuller, Robert H., 55
self-confidence, 21
self-defeat, 55
self-triumph, 55
self-worth, 21, 55
student-athletes, 31-34, 39-45, 47-51

T.
Tar Heels, 3, 29, 70
Tennessee Volunteers, 1-2, 56
Twitter, 47

U.
Uncle Henry, 2, 13, 25, 28, 30-31, 69
University of North Carolina (UNC), 3, 10, 28-30, 32-34

and academic misconduct, 41, 44, 48
and football, 4, 7, 10, 36-40
and scholarship, 26-29

V.
Varsity football, 26-27

W.
Watson, Terry, 36
Williams, Adrain, 17
Williams, Doretha Jane, 14-15
    relationship with grandson, 2, 13, 16-17, 19-20, 28, 30-31, 35, 40, 69
Williams, Dave, 14
Williams, Roy, 46
Willingham, Mary, 44-45